Resurrection Matters

Church Renewal
for Creation's Sake

Nurya Love Parish

T0272928

Church |
NEW YORK

Church Publishing
19 East 34th Street
New York, NY 10016
www.churchpublishing.org

The image "The Organizational Ecocycle" found on page 26 is reprinted with permission from *Crisis & Renewal: Meeting the Challenge of Organizational Change* by David K. Hurst (Brighton, MA: Harvard Business Press Books, 2002). Copyright 2002 by David K. Hurst; all rights reserved.

Cover design by Jennifer Kopec, 2Pug Design
Typeset by Rose Design

Library of Congress Cataloging-in-Publication Data

Names: Parish, Nurya Love, author.
Title: Resurrection matters : church renewal for creation's sake / Nurya Love Parish.
Description: New York : Church Publishing, 2018. | Includes bibliographical references.
Identifiers: LCCN 2017057962 (print) | LCCN 2018014343 (ebook) | ISBN 9781640650152 (ebook) | ISBN 9781640650145 (pbk.)
Subjects: LCSH: Church renewal. | Jesus Christ—Resurrection. | Ecotheology. | Church renewal—Episcopal Church.
Classification: LCC BV600.3 (ebook) | LCC BV600.3 .P36 2018 (print) | DDC 253—dc23
LC record available at https://lccn.loc.gov/2017057962

Printed in Canada

With thanks to God for inspiring Scnobia Taylor
to give her family's land for reconciliation

For Scnobia's "yes" to God's call
and for the ripple effect of that gift,
which reached and changed my life

For my family—past, present, and future
especially Sherry, David, Claire, and Nathan

For Michael and Bethany Edwardson

And for all who practice resurrection

"The whole material universe is an expression and incarnation of the creative energy of God. . . . For that reason, all good and creative handling of the material universe is holy and beautiful, and all abuse of the material universe is a crucifixion of the body of Christ."

—DOROTHY SAYERS, CREED OR CHAOS?

"Resurrected life, life that participates in the holiness and peace of God, restores creation to its fulness and joy. . . . Resurrection, in other words, becomes the basis for a transformation of culture that will usher in a new song because it teaches us a new way to be alive."

—NORMAN WIRZBA, THE PARADISE OF GOD: RENEWING RELIGION IN AN ECOLOGICAL AGE

Contents

Introduction

What the Church needs, what this world needs, are some Christians who are as crazy as the Lord. Crazy enough to love like Jesus, to give like Jesus, to forgive like Jesus, to do justice, love mercy, walk humbly with God—like Jesus. Crazy enough to dare to change the world from the nightmare it often is into something closer to the dream that God dreams for it. And for those of us who would follow him, those of us who would be his disciples, those of us who would live as the people of the Way? It might come as a shock, but those of us called to that life are called to craziness, too.

—PRESIDING BISHOP MICHAEL CURRY[1]

I was pretty sure I was crazy the day I handed over $15,000, ten acres, and the keys to my house to fulfill God's dream.

Cofounding Plainsong Farm wasn't what I had planned for my life. But God started murmuring to me about this ministry in the early years of the twenty-first century. God whispered about the renewal of discipleship integrated with the care of Creation. God called me toward creating a farm where people could reflect on scripture, be encouraged in spiritual growth, and engage in the practices of sustainable agriculture.

It was a lovely fantasy, but hardly practical. And I could ignore a whisper.

By 2008 God had turned up the volume. Now the call was coming clearly. As I began to hear it more fully, I started speaking to others about this vision for ministry. Back then, I cried every time I talked about it. I thought this meant it might be important. I remembered hearing in seminary that tears were once understood as a sign of the

Holy Spirit. But my doubts about my sanity were quickly reinforced when I shared the dream for Plainsong Farm with others. Every member of my small clergy group—and our leader—gave me a blank stare. I talked with my spiritual director; he appeared puzzled. These were professionals at hearing from God and responding. Surely they knew more than I did. I buried the call once more.

I was resistant, but God is patient. However, God knows how to turn up the volume. By 2013 I could not pray without hearing, loudly and insistently, the call to begin Plainsong Farm. That's when I realized that I was afraid to die without trying. I didn't want to have that conversation with my Lord. That's when I began to pray the prayers that led to the founding of Plainsong Farm.

God brought the farm into being; I didn't. We wouldn't be here at all without divine intervention. And we still barely exist. In our start-up phase, we learned that any farm has to get ten years under its belt before it has a solid foundation. So this isn't the story of *how* Plainsong Farm began, because we're still beginning. This is the story of *why* Plainsong Farm began. Even though I thought I might be crazy, I can now see rationality behind the call—logic based on Holy Scripture and contemporary organizational change theory. That logic wasn't apparent to my clergy group or my spiritual director. That is why the church needs this book.

As I faced forward into the dream of the farm, I couldn't see why a farm-based ministry made sense. Only in hindsight has it become clear: this new beginning occurred *both* because of preparation God provided over twenty years of reading, ministry practice, *and* the crazy willingness to leap. My husband and I turned over the keys to our house, our barns, and the use of our ten acres to a family we barely knew. My cofounders and I self-funded a ministry start-up; we worked without pay while we tried to bring a dream to life. I left a perfectly good, compensated ministry role with a perfectly wonderful congregation just because I couldn't juggle it all anymore.

I thank God for the call of our presiding bishop naming the need for crazy Christians. We do need some crazy Christians. I might qualify.

But in all honesty, I don't think I'm faithful enough to have taken all those steps without a solid foundation in the teachings of scripture, the church, and change theory. I needed to understand *why* God was asking me to take a leap before I was ready to jump. And I needed to know that I wasn't alone.

My guess is that God is whispering in a lot of hearts these days. Both church and Creation are in trouble. The church gets smaller and older every year; the planet gets warmer.

God called both Creation and church into being; God created and loves us. God is acting for us in ways that might not yet be visible—because we humans might not yet see how to bring God's dream to life.

Why would I think that God's dreams for humanity are not yet visible? Because fourteen years passed between the time I first wrote the words "Plainsong Farm" and when the farm actually began. Fourteen years. God's dream was alive long before I was bold enough to act on it. I wrote this book to pass on the lessons that prompted me to take that leap so it doesn't take you—or your church—that long to begin whatever God is whispering about to you.

This book is for both Christians seeking to grow as disciples, and people curious about how Christians think and act for the health of our communities and all Creation. My goal is to take you on a journey that goes from death to life, from decline to renewal, from despair to hope. If you are reading this book as part of your practice of faith, my desire is that this isn't a journey you take alone, but with others. My dream is that you would read this book in communities that already exist: a clergy group, a church book group, a judicatory staff. My prayer is that God would use these words to equip, encourage, and enable more of God's people to live God's dream. Are you troubled by the news about climate change and the decline of the church? Do you wonder what you might do to make a difference? I hope this book helps you find your next answer and, even more, to take your next action.

To become a crazy Christian takes a leap of faith. Before you jump, you need to be able to trust that there is a reason to leave solid ground. God might be calling you—just as God called me for more than a decade—but resistance is normal. Sometimes you need a reason to propel you in the direction where faith leads you. My hope is that these pages provide you both the inspiration to be a crazy Christian and the logic to recognize that taking one next step as a crazy Christian is the sanest thing you can do.

Nurya Love Parish
November 22, 2017
Feast of Clive Staples Lewis

PRELUDE
RELIGION MATTERS

I often say I grew up without any religion. I went to worship at a church precisely once during the first nineteen years of my life. I never went to other houses of worship at all. Neither of my parents found organized religion meaningful. If I wanted to practice faith, they decided, I could figure that out for myself later on.

I was an only child, and a reflective one. In the absence of religious teachings, I found meaning in abstract concepts: compassion, integrity, justice. These were untethered from ancient stories and traditions, which made me feel untethered too. As a college student I found myself looking for someone, somewhere, who had thought through my questions already: how am I to live? what is right? what is good? Slowly it dawned on me that religion was the container for these questions—and their answers.

Because I was born and raised in Las Vegas, Nevada, at an early age I began to realize that humanity was headed for some type of ecological crisis. As a child I recognized that green lawns could not last forever in the desert, and wondered how my species had gone so wrong. More important, how could we be put right again? Eventually, I discovered that religion was the discipline through which these questions had been asked and answered throughout the ages. I converted from "nothing" to "something" because I needed the wisdom of those who had gone before me. I became a Christian and was baptized at the age of twenty-five because in Jesus I found someone worth trusting with my whole life.

Organized religions are meant to be deeply trustworthy. At its core, religion exists to provide a shared language for that which renders us speechless. Organized religion enables the practice of faith—trusting our lives to the One who is far greater than we are—across every generation. As Phyllis Tickle wrote in *The Great Emergence*, religion is like the rope that connects the boat to the shoreline: a "cable of meaning"[1] which tethers us to the source of life. Dr. Cornel West says, "Faith is stepping out on nothing and landing on something."[2] Religion is what teaches us that the first step into "nothing" leads to life and not—as we would logically expect—to death.

The church's crisis and the climate crisis share the same root—a failure to practice the faith that is in us. God's people have always been distracted from relationship with God; this story begins in Genesis, chapter two. Trespassing against God's boundaries because we want to be like God is apparently what we do. Many generations have preserved this story. But preserving the story does not mean we understand what it means for our time.

When it became clear that extracting fossil fuels from the depths of the earth was leading to the destruction of Creation, Christians could have recalled the story of the apple in Eden. We could have remembered that we tend to reach for that which makes us more like God but is actually out of bounds. We could have called for research into the consequences of fossil fuel use. We could have demanded public policy that would steward Creation as witness to God's glory and a home for future generations. We could have made the health of God's world our first priority. If we had done so, we would have witnessed to the importance of remembering scripture as a source of wisdom, while also turning to science as a source of fact. We would have rewoven the cable of meaning that is fraying in our lifetimes. And perhaps, we could have changed the course of history.

The failure to understand and act on the wisdom of scripture did not jeopardize the health of an entire planet in previous generations. But the last hundred years have brought unprecedented technological advances with the maturing of the industrial age into the digital era. The last hundred years have also brought the rise of a market economy focused on short-term financial gain with no effective means to account for long-term ecological cost. Our loss of wisdom means we see Creation as a natural resource to be plundered. The rise of technology provides us the means to plunder it. Our generally accepted accounting counts Creation's loss as humanity's gain. We tend to think of ourselves as gods and God as absent. This aspect of humanity goes back to the beginning. It may very well be our end.

It is unfashionable in an era of pluralism to claim that the church holds unique power to save. But it is certain that the church exists to connect humanity to our Creator. The church holds language, story, tradition, and ritual that can be effective against idolatry. The church is far from perfect. Many, *many* times in our past we have fallen prey to idolatry ourselves. We have failed to be an obedient church;[3] we have not loved God with our whole heart.[4] But inherent to our core purpose is the language of sin, confession, redemption, absolution, and grace. This language is a gift both the church and the world desperately need to make sense of our current predicament.

We have sinned and fallen short of the grace of God. We have followed too much the devices and desires of our own hearts. As a result, our planet is in peril. The good news is that God, in God's mercy, knows our sinfulness and has provided us a means of salvation in Jesus Christ. We left Eden a long time ago. God came to join us outside its gates. Now, as we turn to Christ and offer our lives for his service, God enables us to become stewards of Creation.

The stewardship of Creation begins with a renewal of religion. Science exists to teach us facts. Religion provides a language of reverence. A language of reverence leads to a practice of reverence. And the practice of reverence—the recognition that each day we walk on holy ground—is what our planet needs.

CHAPTER ONE

Taking Resurrection Seriously

My **first journey** into the decision-making process that shapes my church's governance was at the Episcopal Church's General Convention in 2012. It happened to be in Indianapolis, which was an easy drive away. I was curious: what was this gathering like? I signed up to go as a guest for a portion of the meeting. And that's how I found myself in the visitor's gallery of the House of Deputies on July 10, 2012.

The General Convention of the Episcopal Church is a huge event. It combines more than a thousand people meeting for the church's business—over 800 clergy and laity, and over 300 bishops.[1] Add exhibitors, volunteers, and guests, and it can be overwhelming. I wasn't quite sure how to navigate it, but I wanted to know how my church made decisions. So I spent some time watching the decision-making body where I felt most at home: the House of Deputies, where laity and clergy deliberate and decide on the resolutions that govern our common life. On July 10, while I sat in the gallery, Resolution C-095 (Structural Reform) came before that house.

Imagine a vast room the size of a few soccer fields filled with almost a thousand people. Imagine them all facing one direction, sitting at long tables of eight, looking toward a few raised tables of meeting facilitators, note takers, and parliamentarians. Imagine podiums scattered throughout the room with microphones and cameras. Imagine huge screens with the face of whoever is speaking on that screen—because the room is so large that without a screen, a person's face would be the size of a peanut. Imagine a gallery to the side with another fifty or so people in chairs, watching the floor of the House, where the credentialed voters—elected by their dioceses—make choices for the church's future. I was in that gallery, watching that huge floor of deputies, still wondering how this all worked.

Structural Reform

Resolution C095 (Structural Reform)[2] came before the House of Deputies in the customary way. It was passed by a diocese at their convention, then considered and revised by a legislative committee of General Convention. But even though it went through an ordinary process, it was far from an ordinary resolution. It began, "Resolved . . . that this General Convention believes the Holy Spirit is urging The Episcopal Church to reimagine itself." It called for the appointment of a Task Force "to present the 78th General Convention with a plan for reforming the Church's structures, governance, and administration." And it concluded, "Surely I know the plans I have for you, says the Lord, plans for your welfare and not for harm, to give you a future with hope" (Jer. 29:11).

In the gallery, I leaned forward. What kind of discussion would this be? What would be decided?

Because the House had a time limit, discussion was short. A proposed amendment regarding the makeup of the task force took up most of the time available. Without real conversation on the resolution, it was difficult to tell what might happen. Would a majority of the House of Deputies support the statement that God was calling the church to a new vision? Would the church's leadership embrace creating a task force that could seek to change many established aspects of our common life?

President Bonnie Anderson called for prayer before the vote.[3] The House hushed for communion with God, then took a voice vote.

The "ayes" were resounding. When the "nays" were called, there was silence. Among more than eight hundred people, not a single "nay" was heard.[4] As people realized what had happened, a ripple of surprise went through the crowd. The Episcopal News Service later reported that the vote "stunned deputies and visitors alike."[5]

"The Holy Spirit is urging The Episcopal Church to reimagine itself." In the gallery, I rejoiced. I knew we needed a newly invigorated Episcopal Church—and other newly invigorated churches as well—to serve the work of God in the world.

Conversion Matters

For the first twenty-two years of my life, I didn't know there was a way to be seriously Christian that included a historical reading of scripture, the acceptance of multiple human authors of a divinely inspired Bible, a willingness to be wrong, a recognition of multiple religions as worthy of respect, and an openness to all people using their gifts in leadership. Somehow in my nonreligious childhood I picked up the impression that the vast majority of Christians were narrow-minded bigots who rejected science, believed the Bible fell from the sky as the literal word of God, adhered to it slavishly at the cost of their capacity for critical thinking, promoted the supremacy of white men as the only legitimate leaders, and condemned most of the world to hell.

My parents didn't teach me to think about Christianity this way; these were simply vague impressions I formed as a young person in the 1980s. Because I wasn't raised in any religion, my view of Christianity was from the outside looking in. I could only hear the loudest Christian voices, which were often voices of condemnation. Quieter, more moderate Christian voices existed; they just didn't reach my less than fully attentive ears.

It took going to seminary—a seeker who discovered the Unitarian Universalist Association and was called to ordained ministry—to teach me that there was more than one way to be a Christian. When I entered Harvard Divinity School, I believed in God, but I didn't know what I believed *about* God. By the time I left, I was a baptized Christian. It would take me another decade to become an Episcopalian, in part because I first encountered the Episcopal Church reading books, not talking to people. Reading Madeleine L'Engle got me through high school, but it took another decade before I met any actual people belonging to her faith tradition who talked with me about their religion, much less invited me to church.

My whole conversion story is outside the scope of this book, but one portion is essential. In seminary I was assigned to read *The Death and Resurrection of the Beloved Son: The Transformation of Child Sacrifice in Judaism and Christianity* by Jon D. Levenson (Yale University Press, 1995). Because a distinguished professor who practiced Orthodox Judaism wrote it, I couldn't dismiss it as the work of one of those science-rejecting Christians. I picked it up because I had to finish it for class. By the time I put it down, I was forever changed.

The Death and Resurrection of the Beloved Son is a dense academic tome. I was biblically illiterate in those days. But even with my limited knowledge, it convinced me that the story of death and resurrection is not only the essence of the Christian faith, but is also echoed throughout the Bible. Ishmael, Abraham's first son, and Isaac, his second, both come close to death and are miraculously raised to new life (Gen. 21 and 22). Joseph is cast into the pit and almost killed, then raised for a new and different life in Egypt (Gen. 37). God both requires (Exod. 22:29) and rejects (Deut. 18:9–13) the gift of every first-born son of Israel. There's more besides. Reading Levenson's book I realized for the first time that the death and resurrection of Christ might both fit a pattern and also be that pattern's fulfillment.

That was an entirely new idea. It took time and practice for me to trust it. But as I spent time around people who took the resurrection seriously, I began to believe. My scientific skepticism gave way to literary conviction. Finally I came to realize that the renewal of the church and all Creation begins exactly here: with the resurrection of Jesus Christ from the dead. This is the core story of the Christian faith; we exist to proclaim it. It is indeed good news: if the powers of death could not defeat Christ, then they cannot defeat the Christ's body the church. They cannot defeat all Creation, which exists in and through Jesus Christ (John 1).

Resurrection and Renewal

Today, Christ's body—the church—is in need of renewal. In and through Christ that renewal is already provided. As the church, we need to remember both that resurrection is our core story, and that resurrection—when it happens—is always astonishingly unexpected.

When Mary went to the tomb the Sunday after the crucifixion, she thought she was going to mourn the death of her friend and teacher. She never expected to see him alive, to hear he had been raised, to be sent out to tell a story of life and renewal. All of that was an enormous surprise. After all, every single earthly authority had been arrayed against him. The leaders of Israel and of Rome had conspired to kill him. But they were as nothing against the power of God.

If the resurrection of Jesus Christ from the dead teaches nothing else, it teaches this: God can do what we consider impossible. It's been two thousand years since "He is risen!" was first proclaimed. Over the decades and centuries, the church has lost sight of just how extraordinary those words really are. Sometimes it seems like we take the resurrection for granted: a weekly ritual of remembrance, an annual set of holidays to observe. Maybe because I didn't believe in it for the first half of my life, I still find the resurrection astonishing. Nobody saw Christ exit the tomb. But once the disciples saw and heard that God had acted, Christ was alive, and they had work to do, they counted their lives as worthless compared to the incomparably valuable work of God.

This is the invitation of faith: to trust in the invisible God, whose presence can never be fully seen or comprehended. Not just to trust in the *existence* of a being that cannot be seen, but more—to trust in the *agency* of a being that cannot be seen. And harder still—not just to trust in the agency of a being that cannot be seen—but *to give over your own life* to be used as an agent of that invisible being, that the impossible might be achieved by God, *through you*.

This is faith. Nobody said it would be easy. But if the Holy Spirit is calling the church to reimagine itself, that means God seeks to work in and through us all.

Since the day I finished reading *The Death and Resurrection of the Beloved Son*, I've gone from dismissing the resurrection to making it the core of my life story. As I've done so, I've come to see that it only makes sense day-by-day. Marge Piercy once wrote, "There is no justice we don't make daily, like bread and love."[6] As a disciple of Jesus, I am called daily to die to self and live for God. That means every day is a kind of crucifixion and resurrection, a chance to begin again. Every day we are called to die to self and live to God, whose nature is Love (1 John 4). As God's people baptized into the death and resurrection of Christ, we are first drowned, then reborn as God's holy people.[7] It turns out that this is just the beginning of the life of faith. As Wendell Berry wrote, we are to "practice resurrection."[8]

This doesn't come easily if you are anything like me. It is hard work. It takes practice. The amazing thing is that God really does provide growth and new life when we turn and seek to put God first. The invisible God, through us, bears visible fruit—even against all odds.

As we give our lives to practicing resurrection, we discover the truth that is proclaimed in the ancient prayers of the church: "Christ broke the bonds of death and hell, and rose victorious from the grave."[9]

I trust in the resurrection. I also remember I cannot fully comprehend it. I am human like Mary, lamenting the loss of the ones I love. My church is in decline. All Creation is in trouble. But if resurrection is the cornerstone of my faith, I am called to give my life for the new life God seeks to create through me. If you seek to follow Jesus, that is your calling too.

The church is not an end in itself; the church is a means to an end. The church's mission is to proclaim the gospel and to restore all people to unity with God and each other in Christ.[10] As Norman Wirzba writes, "The clear implication of Christ's cosmic lordship was that the church, the continuing representative of Christ on earth, was to serve as the medium and manifestation of Christ's creative and reconciling work to the whole creation."[11]

Our life of prayer and worship reminds us of the purpose of our lives: as members of God's Creation, to belong fully to our Creator—loving God first and best. As Jesus taught, we are to love God with "all your heart, and with all your soul, and with all your strength, and with all your mind" (Luke 10:27). Worship reminds us who we are, and Whose we are. It knits us back into the fabric of Creation, bringing us into alignment with God as we praise God together. Worship proclaims that every square inch of this planet and every single one of earth's creatures is made by God, belongs to God, and is beloved by God. As we worship, we witness to the reality that we are members of the body of Christ—a body which rose from the grave, a body which crosses all customary boundaries of place and time, a body which is one with all Creation.

As members of the body of Christ, we're in the resurrection business.

We're actually not in the maintenance business.

We are really good at maintaining institutions. It's what we know how to do. The altar guild knows how to tend the sacramental vessels; the choir is great at singing; the treasurer is comfortable preparing financial statements. If someone is new in a role, training is often at hand. The focus is on caring for the work of the church with attentiveness and reverence. There is nothing wrong with that—except that it falls radically short of God's call to us. It is wonderful, as far as it goes. It just doesn't go far enough.

If we are to be agents of reconciliation, participants in the loving, life-giving, liberating work of Jesus, it takes our whole lives. It takes being willing to do what we prefer not to do. Because that's exactly how the resurrection began.

Facing the Cross

The core story we tell as a church—the story of resurrection—begins with crucifixion. It begins with a man in a garden saying, "My Father, if it is possible, let this cup pass from me; yet *not what I want but what you want*" (Matt. 26:39, emphasis mine). We call that man Savior and Lord. We say he is our greatest example. One thing Jesus clearly did in the garden was this: he named out loud, to God, his request to avoid the cross. Then, he accepted that his petition might not be fulfilled.

Jesus knew what was coming. He had known it for a while. He had even tried to share his coming trials with his disciples. But they just didn't get it. When he asks the disciples, "Who do you say that I am?" Peter proclaims, "You are the Messiah, the Son of the living God." A few verses later, Jesus "began to show his disciples that he must go to Jerusalem and undergo great suffering at the hands of the elders and chief priests and scribes, and be killed, and on the third day be raised."

Peter takes him aside and says, "God forbid it, Lord! This must never happen to you." (See Matt. 16:15–23.)

Peter's interaction with Jesus is whiplash-inducing. In one moment he is willing to follow Jesus anywhere. In the next, he's saying "Except not death, Lord!" Peter likes the status quo: crowds, approval, miracles. Who wouldn't? But Jesus knows what is coming. He knows that entering Jerusalem will put him on a collision course with the earthly authorities. He also knows that he must enter Jerusalem, come what may, to complete his life and ministry.

Peter stands in for all of us in this instance. We want to proclaim Jesus Lord and God. But we don't want to follow him to the cross. That sounds and feels terrifying. Nothing in our lives outside the church prepares us for it. The world expects life, health, success, and growth. This is what is praised, acclaimed, and celebrated. But when Christ went to the cross, he was not praised, acclaimed, nor celebrated. He was crucified.

Peter didn't want Jesus talking about such disturbing things, because he didn't want them to be true. But Jesus—the way, the truth, and the life—was committed to seeing and speaking truth, come what may. As disciples of Jesus, we have to be willing to speak and hear hard truths. We are to be more like Jesus than we are like Peter. There are three hard truths we need to acknowledge:

1. The church is dying.
2. The globe is warming.
3. We are called to renew the church and safeguard the integrity of Creation.[12] And we don't know how.

Let's take these truths one by one.

The church is dying. The general data trend is clear: the Episcopal Church is smaller each year. (This is also generally true for the historic mainline Protestant traditions.) In many places the church is also becoming older. Many congregations will close in the next ten years if we continue on our current course. Dioceses, questioning their financial viability, will shrink and merge. Already, church members are quietly wondering whether their community of faith will last another five or ten years—but are often afraid to ask those questions out loud. Our clergy, bishops, and General Convention deputies know that demographic data indicate a tsunami of church closings is at hand, but the capacity of church leaders to openly discuss this situation varies significantly from place to place and person to person. Silence and denial about our situation does not make it any less perilous. In some regions of the country, church closings are no big deal; there are enough churches, close together, to ensure ample provision for common worship and sacramental ministry. Where I live, however, a single church closing can mean an entire county is without an Episcopal presence. In many places, the situation is critical.

The globe is warming. The general data trend is clear: the climate is warmer each year. In many places it is also less stable. If we continue on our current course, the seas will rise and coastal communities will be driven inland. Climate-related migration has already begun. Already, individuals are quietly wondering how their grandchildren will cope someday as adults in a changed climate—but are often afraid to ask these questions out loud. Our elected leaders, scientists, and the global community know that temperature data indicate extraordinary shifts in ecosystems are likely, but the public capacity to discuss this situation varies significantly from place to place, political party to political party, and person to person. Silence and denial about our situation does not make it any less perilous. There is nowhere on the globe that will not be affected by climate change, but communities which are already vulnerable—poorer communities, island nations—are losing their capacity to survive in their current location. In many places, the situation is critical.

We are called to renew the church and safeguard the integrity of Creation. And we don't know how. The parallels in the two above descriptions are intentional. The crisis in church and Creation mirror each other. Both the church and the planet are the work of God. Each are called into existence by God; the Holy Spirit breathes through each. The church, the body of Christ in the world, is meant to thrive; all Creation, which was made through Christ, is meant to thrive. God desires life and health for the church and all Creation. But that's not where we are. And we don't quite seem to know how to get where we belong.

Risk for the Sake of the Gospel

If we knew how to stop the decline of the church and the warming of the globe, we would have done it already. But despite many efforts to halt both trends, they continue. Many people work tirelessly for the stewardship and renewal of the church; many people work tirelessly for political and scientific solutions to climate change. But the data continue to accumulate year after year: smaller church, warmer planet. One day—we know not when, and perhaps not even during our lifetimes—these trends will halt and reverse. But we can't predict that day. Even less can we predict what chaos and sadness will arrive before it does.

If we are Easter people, we can face hard truths in a way that Peter—before the resurrection—could not. We know that we already have a risen Savior; we know that God does not intend the death of the church or the planet. And we know that denying the difficult does not make it go away. On the contrary: only as we face into the truths before us can we find our way through them. If they are too hard for us to face on our own, that's fine, because we aren't on our own. We are in Christ.

I had to die to my notion of what a normal ministry career would include in order to begin Plainsong Farm. I had to die to my expectation for a normal salary. I had to die to my desire to understand and manage my own life. These are not small things to let go. But Jesus tells his disciples, "If any want to become my followers, let them deny themselves and take up their cross daily and follow me. For those who want to save their life will lose it, and those who lose their life for my sake will find it" (Luke 9:23–24).

And that is true. As Matt Overton, a youth ministry innovator, writes, "I knew that if the American church was ever going to be born again in the twenty-first century, it would need people willing to risk everything for kingdom ideas that were worth their very blood, sweat and tears. The church needed to start swinging for the fences. . . . The gospel is, at its core, a risky proposition by God in behalf of human beings. It promises no security, despite our best attempts to deify security and regularity in our worshipping communities."[13]

If the resurrection is the core of our faith, then ordinary maintenance mode just won't do. We serve an amazing God and God provides a means for us to be amazing witnesses. "Glory to God in the highest and peace to his people on earth" are not just a few words we recite at the beginning of the Sunday liturgy; they are a way of life. To glorify God we must be willing to let go of the familiar and trust that God will lead us. Taking resurrection seriously means acknowledging the real, hard truths that are before us, proclaiming that Christ is risen, and asking God to do a new thing through us. We are called to trust in the invisible to achieve the impossible—against all odds.

If there is any group on earth that has the wisdom needed for a warming planet, it is the people of God who steward the ancient words and rituals that show the way when there is no way. The Holy Spirit is calling the church to reimagine itself. We begin at the beginning: in the face of death and despair, we proclaim resurrection.

INTERLUDE
A MEMORIAL TO THE CHURCH

In the months leading up to the General Convention of 2015, an open letter (or "memorial") to the church was written and shared widely online. It was initially authored by a small group of seven people who invited others to sign on as they felt moved. Thirty-three bishops, a hundred thirty deputies, alternates, and official youth representatives, and almost four hundred Episcopalians added their names as signatories to this document.

It still speaks to us today.

A Memorial to the Church[1]

To the Deputies and Bishops of The Episcopal Church assembled at the 78th General Convention:

> Now those who were scattered went from place to place, proclaiming the word. Philip went down to the city of Samaria and proclaimed the Messiah to them. The crowds with one accord listened eagerly to what was said by Philip, hearing and seeing the signs that he did. So there was great joy in that city. *Acts 8:4–6, 8*

In the eighth chapter of the Acts of the Apostles, the newly formed church of disciples of the risen Savior found itself in a new situation. No longer could Christians depend on traditional ways of following

Jesus and traditional places in which to do it. Driven out of their comfortable existence praying in the Temple in Jerusalem and waiting for the kingdom to come, they found themselves in new and unexpected neighborhoods, developing new ways of proclaiming the Word. Yet they found that the crowds were eager to hear the Good News of Christ and welcomed it with joy. The very loss of the old ways of being the church gave them opportunities to expand and multiply the reach of Christ's loving embrace.

Our beloved Episcopal Church is in a similar situation. We must find new ways of proclaiming the gospel in varied and ever changing neighborhoods. Old ways of being the church no longer apply. We can no longer settle for complacency and comfort. We can no longer claim to dominate the political and social landscape. We can no longer wait inside our sanctuaries to welcome those who want to become Episcopalian.

We have a choice before us. We can continue, valiantly and tragically, to try to save all the rights and privileges we have previously enjoyed. We can continue to watch our church dwindle until it someday becomes an endowed museum to the faith of our forebears. We can continue business as usual until we lose our common life entirely.

Or we can lose our life for Jesus' sake so that we might save it.

We, the undersigned, hold dear the Episcopal Church and believe passionately in the gift this church offers. Washed in the waters of Baptism and nourished from the deep springs of word and sacrament, we experience the power of God's presence as we open the Scriptures and celebrate the Eucharist. We stand in awe of the mystery of the Holy Trinity and the power of the triune God to love, to forgive, to make whole. We know the joy of serving God through serving others. We long for a world with every unjust structure toppled. We love this church enough to yearn for it to be transformed.

We recognize the importance of this present moment. We join the Task Force for Reimagining the Church in calling for the church to follow Jesus into the neighborhood, traveling lightly. Our deepest hopes and aspirations are not dependent upon any particular act of this Convention. Many essential steps are found in the daily walk of discipleship undertaken by congregations and individuals throughout the church, and we commend the work of many who are helping the church adopt these discipleship practices. This Convention, however, has the opportunity to act on a number of matters that can support God's faithful people, our parishes and missions, and our dioceses in living out the Great Commission and the Great Commandment.

Specifically, we call upon the people of the Episcopal Church to:

- Recommit to reading scripture, praying daily, gathering weekly for corporate worship, and giving for the spread of the Kingdom, knowing that engaging in these practices brings personal and corporate transformation;
- Share the Good News of Jesus Christ in word and deed, including learning how to tell the story of how Jesus makes a difference in our lives, even and especially to those who have not experienced true transformation;
- Pray and fast for the Holy Spirit to add day by day to those who come within the reach of Christ's saving embrace;
- Encounter Jesus Christ through loving service to those in need and through seeking justice and peace among all people.

And we call upon those bishops and deputies gathered for Convention to the following actions as specific ways we may enter this time of transition in a spirit of exploration, discovering the gifts that the Holy Spirit has for us in this moment:

- Engage creatively, openly, and prayerfully in reading the signs of the times and discerning the particular ways God is speaking to the Episcopal Church now;

- Pray, read the scriptures, and listen deeply for the Holy Spirit's guidance in electing a new Presiding Bishop and other leaders, in entering into creative initiatives for the spread of the kingdom, and in restructuring the church for mission;
- Fund evangelism initiatives extravagantly: training laborers to go into the harvest to revitalize existing congregations and plant new ones; forming networks and educational offerings to train and deploy church planters and revitalizers who will follow Jesus into all kinds of neighborhoods; and creating training opportunities for bilingual and bi-cultural ministry;
- Release our hold on buildings, structures, comfortable habits, egos, and conflicts that do not serve the church well;
- Remove obstacles embedded in current structures, however formerly useful or well-meaning, that hinder new and creative mission and evangelism initiatives;
- Refocus our energies from building up a large, centralized, expensive, hierarchical church-wide structure, to networking and supporting mission at the local level, where we all may learn how to follow Jesus into all of our neighborhoods.

Like those early followers of Christ, we find ourselves being scattered out of familiar and comfortable places and ways of being the church. Rather than be ruled by memory and consumed by fear, we can embrace this crisis, trusting that the Lord of Life will give us everything we need to spread the Gospel, proclaim the kingdom, and share the love of God. May God grant great joy in every city and neighborhood into which we go.

Respectfully submitted,

Susan Brown Snook, Tom Ferguson, Scott Gunn, Frank Logue, Brendan O'Sullivan-Hale, Steve Pankey, Adam Trambley

CHAPTER TWO

The Ecology of Renewal

I t was 1990 when God first called me to ministry. I was nine-teen and still functionally agnostic; God called me before I knew God. I still remember rationalizing that it would be fine for me to follow this extremely unexpected call. I thought, "Ministry is a solid career path. The church is a stable institution. I can still have a respectable life."

The twenty-first century wrecked every one of those assumptions. Ministry is not a solid career path when young seminarians are now advised to prepare for bivocational ministry.[1] As buildings are sold and dioceses ponder merger, the church is not a particularly stable institution. In western Michigan, it's still respectable to be a clergyperson. In much of the rest of America, telling someone you're a pastor is almost guaranteed to get you at least an awkward pause in the conversation and occasionally a stopped conversation altogether.

Time for the Rummage Sale

As the church has grappled with these trends, no one has done more to give us a language and concepts for our time in history than Phyllis Tickle. Her book *The Great Emergence* named the extraordinary shifts taking place in our lifetimes. The catch phase that many took away from her work was the concept of the "rummage sale." As she wrote (quoting the Rt. Rev. Mark Dyer), "the only way to understand what is currently happening to us as twenty-first century Christians in North

America is first to understand that about every five hundred years the church feels compelled to hold a giant rummage sale. . . . [T]he empowered structures of institutionalized Christianity . . . become an intolerable carapace that must be shattered in order that renewal and new growth may occur."[2]

When Phyllis began speaking about the "rummage sale" cycle, the church finally had usable language for the extraordinary shifts taking place in our time. We might not know why our institutions are in decline, but we know what a rummage sale is. Finding that metaphor was a necessary step toward a faithful response to our current situation.

But, helpful as it is, the rummage sale analogy is not the greatest gift that *The Great Emergence* provides us. With her book, Phyllis did her best to teach us that the changes we were experiencing weren't *about* us. The decline of mainline America was part of a larger cultural shift. Nobody was controlling it, and it affected every single sector of society. Publishing and higher education were having their own rummage sales. The church wasn't alone in this, and it wasn't our fault. The time had simply come for us to reconsider, regroup, and seek renewal.

In *The Great Emergence*, Phyllis named the core function of religion as a meaning-making apparatus. She pointed out that the "cable of meaning" had broken as a result of the scientific discoveries of the 1800s—which had slowly but surely made their way into popular consciousness. She pointed to Darwin, Faraday, Freud, Jung, and Campbell. She cited Einstein and Schweitzer. She described the impact of radio, television, and the world wide web. She considered the shifts in family roles and the impact of women's participation in the industrial economy's paid workforce. She made it clear that the institutions of religion are being changed in our lifetimes because of a widespread cultural re-examination of fundamental principles of our society.

In a highly networked, technology-driven age, Phyllis told us, the institutions born in the age of Reformation—nation-states trading by means of a capitalist economy—are no longer secure in their authority. And neither is Protestant Christianity. As Thomas Friedman told us, *The World Is Flat* (New York: Farrar, Straus, and Giroux, 2005). Why would we expect the forms of our faith to survive as they once were? While everything changes around us, why would our religious institutions remain unchanged? The church is unique in society, but it isn't *that* unique. Our message is eternal, but our structure is temporal.

In the decade since *The Great Emergence* was published, the trends that it describes have only continued. The rummage sale continues, and in fact has expanded. As white Americans come to grips with the killing of African-Americans at the hands of the police, it has become evident that our country's foundational principles are tied up with the lie of white supremacy. The same virtual networks that create community untethered to place also enable the broadcast of news and opinion from the grassroots. Twitter enabled all of America to discover what was happening on the ground when police in Ferguson killed Mike Brown. As DeRay Mckesson, one of the lead social media broadcasters, said, "We didn't discover injustice in August 2014. We did have a different set of tools."[3] That set of tools broke open a new set of questions that are of one piece with the rest of the Great Emergence. How can white Christians trust our churches when we know our ancestors in the faith—and the institutions they stewarded and we now inherit—were complicit in colonialism and slavery? How can we believe in a church that stood for oppression and violence?

Phyllis would tell us that this is all part of the rummage sale. Our era inherits a Christianity that is not only being rethought and reimagined, but also reconstituted incarnationally in our institutions.

We can see that the former things are passing away; we are listening for what God is doing to bring forth new things. The church's existence is not founded on buildings, endowments, jobs, or pension plans; the church's existence is founded on the gift of God's self: the Holy Spirit.

Phyllis Tickle isn't the only person who chronicles the rise and fall of organizations. David K. Hurst is another notable thinker practically unknown to the American church. A business professor in Canada, his book *Crisis & Renewal: Meeting the Challenge of Organizational Change* (Harvard Business Review Press, 1995) is the other handbook to the Rummage Sale Era. It proposes a theory of organizational life that the church would do well to heed in these times.

From Crisis to Renewal: An Ecological Model

Hurst's writing is not grounded in church history or theology; I doubt he intended it to be received by the church at all. (Christians will need to overlook the book's dedication "to the Goddess.") Nevertheless, the model for organizational renewal that Hurst proposes is grounded in natural systems, which themselves reveal the character of God. Hurst's capacity to extrapolate usable organizational theory from enduring ecological principles makes his book required reading for the church today. Where most theories of organizational life begin with the birth of an organization and end with its death, Hurst's model is an infinity loop in which organizational endings are simply precursors to new beginnings—if one is bold enough to take the path that leads from death to life.

I was introduced to David K. Hurst by Curt Bechler, an organizational consultant who arrived at the board meeting of my daughter's Montessori daycare at about the same time I did. I was a new board member; he had been hired to help us get through the mess we were in. His first presentation was Hurst's ecocycle model. As he drew the infinity loop on the board, he described the process of organizational birth, crisis, and renewal. (I didn't record him speaking that day; what follows is my best recollection of his words more than a decade after I first heard them.)[4]

"Say you want to start something new," he began. "You can't do it alone, so you recruit a couple of friends. They agree to work with you." As he talked, he drew:

-

"But you can't do anything until you know what you're doing, so you spend some time getting organized. You meet together to get clear on your vision and your purpose. You do some deep dives into why you're there together."

"After a while it becomes evident that the work will go more smoothly if you have defined roles, so you figure out who does what. Your new organization begins, and starts to offer what you want to provide the public. Good news! The public likes it. You have created something that is accepted, embraced, and valued."

"In fact, it's so well accepted and highly valued that you need to do more of it. You have to scale up—and that means creating systems and processes and finding a way to welcome more people on board so you can get better and bigger at the thing you do. Now there aren't just you and a couple of friends, there are departments and policies and procedures—and all of this is necessary for you to continue to provide this amazing and highly valued something at the scale that it is desired by others."

"And then one day something happens. It might start out as something small. But there's a shift. Instead of everything chugging along with continued external demand and continued internal development, things kind of level off. Then they do more than level off—they actually start to decline."

"At first you can hardly believe it. The upward trend line is so strong and it continued for so long, surely this is just a temporary blip. Surely in a little bit, things will naturally reverse on their own. You don't need to do anything different for now—just wait a bit and your life will be back to normal."

"Except it doesn't get back to normal. The decline continues. It more than continues, it actually accelerates. By this point it becomes clear that you need to change something. The only problem is, you don't know what to change. You start trying things, different things, sometimes it seems like anything. (By the way, this is the point in the loop where some organizations just spiral out and die.)"

"And then, as you're trying all these different things, one of them catches hold. Or maybe a few of them. They start out as small experiments, but they are small experiments that grow out of your existing values. And for some reason—you don't even know why—now these are the things that resonate. Not the old things that you used to do, but these new things that are kind of like the old things but also somehow different. They are close enough to your core capacities that you can offer them; they are close enough to the desires of the wider public that people want them. And so you begin a whole new process of taking apart the systems and processes that you used to need to be able to do the old thing you used to do, and creating new systems and processes to be able to do the new thing you do."

"And what you notice is that it feels a whole lot like starting over—even though your organization already exists, you have to now ask the very same questions you asked in the beginning: what are we doing here? What do we need in order to be able to provide what only we can provide? How should we organize ourselves now and what is the core offering that we can make?"

"A healthy organization," Curt concluded, "will go through this cycle multiple times. The two ends of the loop are where organizations crash and burn. It's easy to quit when you don't know what you're doing. The fun times are when you're riding the curve up: when you know what you're doing, people want what you're doing, and it's time to expand. The challenging times are in that opposite loop, when you're rethinking everything you do as you seek a way to provide value today."

He was there to provide consulting to my daughter's daycare. But that day, I got the model I needed as a minister in the mainline church. I came home and ordered *Crisis & Renewal*. I read it in a single sitting. It spoke to me even more as a single volume in organizational change than it had as a short lecture from a visiting consultant. What Christian in the Rummage Sale Era wouldn't love a book that begins:

> This book is about organizational renewal and the essential role of crisis in the process of renewal. Renewal is concerned with the revival in mature organizations of the values, feelings, excitement, and emotional commitment often experienced only in the beginning of an organization's life. Renewal is about the restoration of something of value, something important, that has been either lost or forgotten as the organization has grown and prospered.[5]

Renewal and Revival

The book of Acts and indeed the entire New Testament communicate the values, feelings excitement, and emotional commitment that was part of the church's early life. Each time of transition in Phyllis Tickle's five-hundred-year retelling of church history led to a renewal of commitment and, as Phyllis describes, an expansion of the proclamation of the gospel. In the most recent past, the church's scale-up stage of the post–World War II era, when religion was part and parcel of civic society, engendered commitment and excitement for the institutional embodiment of the message of Jesus. But there is nothing clearer in the twenty-first century than the need for revival in the mature organization of the church.

So how does it work?

Although Hurst draws on examples from Quaker history and the steel industry, the heart of his book is an explanation of a forest system ecocycle. He identifies four phases in the life cycle of a forest:

1. **Exploitation**, in which newly available space (for example, through the fall of a large tree) is rapidly colonized by fast-growing plants seeking additional access to sunlight;

2. **Conservation**, in which slower-growing plants move in and displace the fast-growing plants to create a tightly connected, somewhat stable ecosystem—a stable or "climax" forest;

3. **Creative Destruction**, in which fire arrives and destroys—as part of a process of renewal—a portion of this stable system;

4. **Mobilization and Renewal**, in which loosely connected regenerative processes combine to bring new life from the old seeds left behind by the prior forest's mature trees.

As Hurst makes clear, this isn't a one-time experience; this is a cycle repeated over and over in nature from time immemorial. He builds his entire ecocycle theory of organizational life upon it.

Hurst's ecocycle loop has two major planes. There is a forward loop, which is focused on performance. In this part of the cycle, the organization knows what it is doing and is seeking simply to get bigger and better. There is a backward loop, which is focused on learning. In this part of the cycle, the organization has experienced some type of crisis and is seeking a renewed version of itself. Both cycles are necessary to develop strong, resilient organizations. In fact, Hurst argues that just as forests require fires, organizations require crises in order to maintain health.

The figure on page 26 shows the stages of a mature organization's life according to Hurst's *Crisis & Renewal*. Although they are marked with numbers, these are simply chosen to enable points of discussion.[6]

Interestingly, any organization begins with what Hurst marks as number 8: entrepreneurial action. Perhaps it is marked as the last rather than the first number in the cycle to remind readers that every entrepreneurial action begins with the seeds harvested from another generation's fruitfulness. The second stage of strategic management

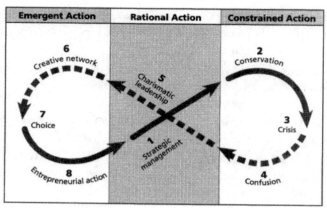

Emergent Action	Rational Action	Constrained Action

6 Creative network
5 Charismatic leadership
2 Conservation
7 Choice
1 Strategic management
3 Crisis
8 Entrepreneurial action
4 Confusion

The Organizational Ecocycle[7]

is the growth and performance cycle as expansion occurs in response to interest and energy. But as the organization reaches mature life, the natural impulse is to conserve resources rather than to risk them on new initiatives. That mission drift leads to crisis and confusion. In order for the new seeds for the future to be discovered and planted, what Hurst terms "charismatic leadership" must occur. He defines charismatic leadership as "values-based rationality—action taken for its intrinsic worth in demonstrating deeply held beliefs about human relationships."[8] As Hurst defines charismatic leaders, they naturally seek out and support others. Together, their creative networks enable new activities and a new cycle of performance to begin.

Crisis & Renewal neatly supports a cyclical reading of the church's history if read together with *The Great Emergence*. Hurst makes clear that at any time, some portion of every mature and complex ecosystem is undergoing creative destruction and renewal. In an organization as large, complex, and uncoordinated as the international, multidenominational body of Christ, the American mainline is simply a sector undergoing creative destruction at our time in history. Simply put, we are in the crisis stage of the ecocycle model.

So what do we do about it? What is the work of the back end of the ecocycle?

According to Hurst and other organizational theorists, every lasting organization is built on a foundation of enduring values. Although its specific form and offerings may change, its values are unchanging. When it is clear the old ways are crumbling, and the organization seeks a new path—there are two steps that lead toward new life: 1) get really clear on the organization's purpose and values; 2) figure out—often through trial and error—how to embody that purpose and those values in a way that meets the needs of the time. The seeds for new life are found by searching for the heart of the organization's past growth. Those seeds contain the organization's DNA, its essence.

This book starts with the resurrection because there can be no doubt that the church's origin story is the life, death, and resurrection of Jesus Christ. Because Christ was raised from the dead and we are members of his body, we too are raised with him to newness of life (Rom. 6:4). Our organization—the church—is empowered for life with the very breath of God, the Holy Spirit.

The church is spending far too much time lamenting the loss of what is passing away. "I am about to do a new thing; now it springs forth, do you not perceive it?" (Isa. 43:19). If we are to be true to our founder, Jesus Christ, our focus must be on seeking the "new thing" God is doing. And that means all of us—laity and clergy both. We are all needed, across all orders of ministry, across all geographic locations, across local churches both big and small. Each disciple of Jesus has a unique vantage point on the church's mission and ministry in their specific context.

Hurst makes clear that when an organization is on the "learning loop" rather than the performance loop, organizations that expect their hierarchy to have all the answers struggle longer. The more active minds called to the task of learning, the more potential solutions can be considered and tried. When an organization is on the performance loop, its hierarchy can manage known processes to drive performance forward. But the job changes when an organization is on the learning loop. In that situation, the hierarchy must model behavior that aligns with core values, remind the organization of its essential purpose and create processes that enable everyone to learn together. That is our current task.

There can be no doubt that the mainline church in twenty-first-century America has passed the performance loop in the ecocycle model. The median age of the American public is thirty-eight years old,[9] but in almost three-quarters of Episcopal congregations over half of the membership is age fifty or over.[10] It is clear that younger generations are not finding meaning and purpose in our current forms and structures. And yet the human need for meaning, purpose, and community—all of which are found through participation in religious life—is unchanging from one generation to the next. Jesus Christ is the same yesterday, today, and forever (Heb. 13:8).

It is God's desire to make a new generation of disciples. Our Rummage Sale Era task is to discern what of our current life is seed—essential to carry on the DNA of our organization to the future—and what is compost—no longer alive in itself, but able to nourish life in the future. That task's urgency is not due to our own alarming rate of church decline. Rather, the urgency of the task rests in the reality that the wider world needs a vibrant, clear, on-message church to meet its own—much larger—crisis.

INTERLUDE
LEARNING TO LISTEN

The Great Emergence was launched into the world in 2008 in celebratory fashion at a conference at St. Mary's Episcopal Cathedral in Memphis. People—many young adults—came from all over the country. Then thirty-seven years old, I was among them. I wanted to be part of the work of God Phyllis Tickle had described when I met her the year before at a church conference in Michigan.

As participants signed in, we received rummage sale tags to use as our conference nametags. We gathered in the vast nave to listen to plenary speakers and to pray. A screen at the front introduced me to Twitter by showing live tweets with the conference hashtag. Nadia Bolz-Weber read to us from her first book, *Salvation on the Small Screen*. And Phyllis spoke to us about the changes in the wider culture and in Christian life.

During one of the early breaks I met the Rev. Tom Brackett, the Episcopal Church's Missioner for Church Planting and Redevelopment, while sitting in the pews. I was a new Episcopalian and found myself telling him that I was wondering if God wanted me to start a farm ministry. Tears welled up in my eyes as I described this call. Tom loaned me his handkerchief and listened. In those days the farm seemed impossible. Tom was the first person who treated it like something that could happen.

As the conference continued, I met people I had never imagined meeting—evangelicals from the west, United Methodists from the south, Episcopalians from the north. All of us were on fire with the sense that God was doing something in our midst. As the gathering drew to an end, I went up to Phyllis and said, "This was a great time of learning, but I feel like we need another gathering for discernment. I think we need a time to pray and seek where Christ is calling us at this time." Her eyes lit up and she said, "Go for it! And keep me posted."

I checked in with some of my newly met companions and they agreed to talk by conference call to see if we could create another gathering. We met regularly for a few months before the financial realities of creating a conference became evident. Together we concluded that it just couldn't happen. After writing to Phyllis with the good news that people were talking about how to create a time for shared discernment, I had to write her with the news that it wasn't feasible. She understood.

It's been a decade since the Memphis *Great Emergence* gathering. As I look back, I realize I failed God, both at that gathering and afterward. My failure wasn't my lack of capacity to create a conference focused on common discernment. At the time, I thought that was failure, but I was wrong. What is clear to me now is that I failed at my own discernment. Even as I listened to myself describe the dream of a farm where people could discover their place in Creation, even with the encouragement of my denomination's officer for new ministry, I didn't yet trust that God could be doing something in or through me.

It would be another five years before I began to take that call seriously.

CHAPTER THREE

Things Fall Apart

I didn't expect being a chaperone on my son's fifth grade history field trip to clarify my perspective on climate change, but that's exactly what happened. We live in Michigan, where Greenfield Village hosts a major museum and living history exhibit. We also live in a school district that is funded to provide every fifth grader a visit there.

In the early 1900s, Henry Ford—the industrialist who founded the Ford Motor Company and one of the wealthiest men of his age—became a collector of artifacts from America's early industrial era. He began by amassing objects from Thomas Edison's lab. Then he built a museum that would "give people a true picture of the development of the country. That's the only history that is worth observing, that you can preserve in itself. We're going to build a museum that's going to show industrial history."[1]

The Henry Ford Museum of American Innovation is now one of the largest indoor-outdoor museums in the United States.[2] It comprises not only a huge indoor museum with examples of early American industrialism—literally trains, planes, and automobiles, along with agricultural equipment—but also a sprawling outdoor village museum with replica homes, stores, and farms from different eras in American life. It has the original lab of Thomas Edison, restored and preserved, plus much more.[3]

It's a great field trip for fifth graders because it brings history to life. And it was a great field trip for me to chaperone. Through it I stumbled across a simple exhibit that helped me place our current climate crisis in context.

From Horse to Horseless Carriage

We were walking down a road in Greenfield Village when I saw it: the "Henry Ford Kitchen Sink Engine Replica." It was a little exhibit on wheels attended by a single staff person. While I watched, he started up an engine small enough I could have held it in my hands. Then he explained it to everyone watching: "Fuel is being sent into this little chamber, where it is mixed with air and combusted from the spark and the plug that pushes the piston. And when the piston pushes out, the exhaust is vented out this little pipe. So it's this continuous motion."[4]

I have zero background in engineering, so even this very basic explanation seemed like a foreign language to me. What did make sense—suddenly, in a way it never had before—was the historical context of the development of the automobile.

Just a couple hundred years ago, most people had no idea how to build a working internal combustion engine, nor did they know how to create an assembly line turning out thousands of automobiles daily. But as many people engaged in small experiments toward building a "horseless carriage," the course of history was changed forever.

Henry Ford was an engineer for the Edison Electric Illuminating Company when he tested his very first internal combustion engine. He tried it out in his own kitchen sink on Christmas Eve, 1893. He wired it to the electric light socket for ignition, and his wife Clara hand-fed it fuel. There was no infrastructure for his work beyond the simple basics of his own home and family. His experiment was what we might call a "side hustle"—his employer didn't sponsor it. It would take ten years from that kitchen sink experiment to the beginnings of the Ford Motor Company, and another five for the first Model T to roll off the line.

As I stood there in 2015 with climate change on my mind, I could only be amazed that the beginnings of the widespread use of the internal combustion engine looked so small. Ford and his contemporaries in the automobile industry had gone on to revolutionize American transportation. There were tremendous short-term benefits in wealth, convenience, and mobility. But there were tremendous costs as well, even in the short term.

One of the people who lived through the change from horse to horseless carriage was Laura Ingalls Wilder. In 1917 she wrote:

A few days ago with several others, I attended the meeting of a woman's club in a neighboring town. We went in a motor car, taking less than an hour for the trip on which we used to spend three hours before the days of motor cars; but we did not arrive at the time appointed nor were we the latest comers by any means. Nearly everyone was late, and all seemed in a hurry. . . .

What became of the time the motor car saved us? Why was everyone late and in a hurry? I used to drive leisurely over to this town with a team, spend a pleasant afternoon, and reach home not much later than I did this time, and all with a sense of there being time enough, instead of a feeling of rush and hurry. We have so many machines and so many helps, in one way and another, to save time; and yet I wonder what we do with the time we save. Nobody seems to have any![5]

On a cold December night in 1893, neither those future benefits nor costs were evident to Henry and Clara Ford. As they stood in their kitchen, all they could see was a small experiment that worked—an experiment so small it would need another decade of dedicated side-hustle tinkering before it began to bear fruit. Christmas Eve gave them the encouragement to keep going.

Now, of course, scientists have determined that the long-term consequences of the widespread adoption of the internal combustion engine, along with the other great discoveries of the industrial age, have placed much of life on our planet in jeopardy. Henry and Clara Ford would have been appalled even to consider that possibility. It was nowhere in their imaginations as they exulted over the newfound wonder in their kitchen sink. But with over a hundred years' hindsight, we can clearly trace the path from the Ford's 1893 Kitchen Sink Engine to Al Gore's 2006 documentary, *An Inconvenient Truth*, where—like so many other Americans—I received my first exposure to the science of climate change.

That path reflects the upward trajectory in David Hurst's theory of organizational development outlined in *Crisis & Renewal*. A small experiment—the Kitchen Sink Engine—receives attention and energy, because it is seen to meet the need of the present day. Due to that awareness and enthusiasm, it continues to develop in order to be offered to the public. An organization is created to steward this process. Early offerings garner wide notice; therefore, the organization grows to meet demand. A system develops to improve and replicate those early offerings: in this case, the development of the assembly line and the widespread production of the Model T. In the case of the horseless carriage, multiple companies produced multiple versions of automobiles, all dependent on the internal combustion engine. In the long run, the entire country shifted to this mode of transportation.

It became clear that a crisis was at hand just a generation later. Pollution clouded the sky in major urban areas. Data began to emerge about human-caused climate change. The Environmental Protection Agency estimates that the transportation sector—the direct descendant of that Kitchen Sink Engine—contributes nearly 30 percent of all greenhouse gases today.[6]

Over the last hundred years, the entire culture of the United States and other developed nations has shifted due to the outcomes of the Industrial Revolution. We take our fossil-fuel-based economy for granted. To be alive in much of the Northern Hemisphere at the beginning of the twenty-first century is to rely on the Industrial Revolution's outcomes for the necessities of life. The majority of our food supply—which was produced without the aid of fossil fuels for the entirety of the human experience, until approximately ninety years ago—depends on fossil fuel–based inputs. The shift from horse to tractor made the "get big or get out" farm policy of the 1970s possible. That policy led to the farm crisis of the 1980s, which unsettled our countryside and displaced a generation of farmers. It led as well to the commodity crop system we now have—which has been tied to the crises of climate change, obesity, and rural poverty. While the world was celebrating industrialization's great benefits (and make no mistake, there are many), it was easy to ignore or postpone dealing with its great costs. But as the global temperature creeps higher, those costs become ever clearer.

Stewards of Creation

"Father, forgive them; for they do not know what they are doing" are the words Jesus Christ uttered on the cross (Luke 23:34). They are just as relevant today as humanity crucifies Creation. A generation of enthusiastic innovators did not know what they were doing. They did not know that one small experiment toward the horseless carriage in 1893 would lead to 3.2 trillion miles driven on U.S. roads in 2016, the fifth straight year of increased mileage.[7] But as the twenty-first century unfolds, we cannot claim lack of understanding. The scientific consensus is clear that the way of life ushered in by industrial innovation is ushering out the health of planet Earth.

Today we find ourselves at a point in history not unlike the one in which Henry and Clara Ford found themselves in 1893: a time of transition when "what is next" has yet to fully emerge. Instead of experimenting our way into the Industrial Revolution, it is time to experiment our way beyond it. Many small experiments must be undertaken to create an economy of health and resilience—an economy that reaches past the fossil fuel era. As disciples of Jesus Christ, we know something about new life emerging when all seems lost. Somehow we are all called to undertake an experiment toward a more sustainable future. We cannot expect the master's tools to dismantle the master's house,[8] taught poet-prophet Audre Lorde.

There are many ways forward into a sustainable future, but at its essence our path is twofold. One of these paths is the "new technology" path. Practitioners in this field seek the development of renewable energy sources and manufacturing processes that minimize or eliminate industrial waste and greenhouse gases. The motivating theory is that new technology can eliminate the problems created by old technology. Electric cars, zero-waste production, solar and wind energy, and many other initiatives fall into this path.

The other path is the "ancient wisdom" path. Practitioners in this field seek to recover skills and ways of life that were common in the preindustrial age: growing and preserving their own food, living near work to minimize transportation needs, and relocalizing their purchases to foster a regional economy. This theory calls for a return to practices that predate the Industrial Revolution, therefore minimizing dependence on fossil fuels and helping develop a regenerative economy.

These two paths are not in opposition; they are parallel and complementary. For example, our family's garage holds two plug-in vehicles: a Toyota Prius, which uses both fuel and electricity, and a Nissan Leaf, which is electric-only. We're clearly embracing the "new technology" path. When I commute to work in one of these cars, half the time I am headed to Plainsong Farm, where we feed our neighbors, put plants in the ground with our own hands, and pray together. This is the "ancient wisdom" path. At the farm's main circle driveway, right in front of the big red barn from the 1800s, are solar panels that date from 2007. This is a great illustration of the compatibility of new technology and ancient wisdom. Both are necessary to go forward in a manner that stewards Creation; neither is widespread enough among the population to make a measurable difference in the cooling of the planet.

We don't yet know how a sustainable ecology will emerge in a postindustrial world. There is no easy answer. What we do know is that we need new kitchen sink (and bigger) experiments. Make no mistake—redeveloping the lost local economy skills of our ancestors takes the same kind of trial, error, and experimentation that leaps of technological innovation require. Today we are at the same stage that Henry and Clara Ford were in 1893. Many people, recognizing that change is needed, are carrying out small experiments across the planet. These experiments are taking place across multiple fields: energy, transportation, technology, home economics, local community organizing, and global politics. No matter how many experiments there are, there will always be room for more. When so little is understood about a problem so vast, all willing souls are required. There is no doubt that humanity has entered what Hurst would call the "crisis" stage. The planet cannot endure our current rate of fossil fuel emissions without enormous ecological and human consequences. As a whole—across political parties, and with an eye to finding multiple workable solutions—we must enter the "learning loop" stage together.

The church is uniquely called and equipped to carry out these experiments. Unlike any other segment of society, religious organizations steward a language of reverence for Creation. That language of reverence is vital if we are to move past a mindset that views the earth as a resource to be used, an error of thought that undergirds our present crisis. Religious bodies affirm that the earth is not a morally neutral storehouse of resources to be exploited for material gain, but instead a good (Gen. 1:1), which we humans are called and mandated to steward. The widespread adoption of this mental shift is essential for a vital future on this planet.

What does the church say about Creation and our role in it? We proclaim that all things are created and redeemed through Jesus Christ (John 1:1–3; Col. 1:20). We affirm that we belong to Christ in life and in death (Rom. 14:8). We proclaim that Christ is victorious over death and the grave (1 Cor. 15:56–57). In baptism we renounce the evil powers of this world and the sinful desires that draw us from the love of God. And we promise to proclaim by word and example the Good News of God in Christ.

These are not empty words. They have been passed down to us from our ancestors because they contain power. They connect us to the Creator of the Universe. They enable us to live, through God's grace, in accordance with God's will. Through the gift of the Holy Spirit at baptism, we are empowered to act in God's world on God's behalf. When we promise that our word and example will share the Good News of God in Christ, we dedicate ourselves to living out God's grace. In a world too often enslaved to death and destruction, we offer our lives to proclaim and practice resurrection. And when we forget, and go astray, the Book of Common Prayer is very clear on what we are to do: repent, return to the Lord, and begin again.

Much of the church in North America in the second half of the twentieth century was a handmaiden to the late industrial age. Churches built big buildings and exulted in the outward trappings of success, including big budgets and plenty of staff. We look back to those days with nostalgia. The church was large then. We didn't need to worry about our own survival. But we forget that as we followed the spirit of the age, we trespassed against Creation. While by outward appearances the church was strong, in wisdom we were weak.

Forgive us, Lord, for we did not know what we were doing. Like Peter, we tried to be faithful, but denied our Lord. It took waking up to the harm our grandchildren and great-grandchildren will face on a rapidly warming planet for us to realize the cock had crowed.

Peter is the rock on whom Christ builds his church. Peter made early errors, but recovered to begin again. So can we.

FROM DENIAL
TO DOUGHNUTS

Peter denied Christ not once, not twice, but three times. This man, whom Jesus named "rock." This man, on whom Jesus said he would build his church. This man to whom Jesus said he would give the keys to the kingdom.

When he realized what he had done, the scripture says he "wept bitterly" (Luke 22:62). I think that must minimize his actual feelings. I think he was absolutely devastated by his own behavior. Then, he must have been overcome by shame and incomprehensibly confused. After all, the resurrection was unprecedented. Peter experienced it firsthand. Appalled by himself, amazed and bewildered at the action of God—that's our friend Peter, in whom we are all meant to find ourselves.

And I do find myself in Peter. I find myself in Peter on all the days when I deny what is true, when I deny what matters. When I am too rushed to sit down and pause for lunch because I am in denial about how much time my to-do list will take. When I go to a run-of-the-mill restaurant and order a meat dish, because I am in denial about how that meat was raised. When I allow myself to be overwhelmed by the intricacies of the Farm Bill[1] and the risks of engaging in public policy because I am in denial about my own capacity to make change.

I find myself in Peter on the night of Christ's arrest when I find myself going too fast, playing too small, and closing my eyes to the truth. And that happens every single day.

What Jesus says to me and to us all is the same thing he said to Peter on the beach. He says, "Come and have breakfast."

Just after daybreak, Jesus stood on the beach; but the disciples did not know that it was Jesus. Jesus said to them, "Children, you have no fish, have you?" They answered him, "No." He said to them, "Cast the net to the right side of the boat, and you will find some." So they cast it, and now they were not able to haul it in because there were so many fish. That disciple whom Jesus loved said to Peter, "It is the Lord!" When Simon Peter heard that it was the Lord, he put on some clothes, for he was naked, and jumped into the sea. But the other disciples came in the boat, dragging the net full of fish, for they were not far from the land, only about a hundred yards off.

When they had gone ashore, they saw a charcoal fire there, with fish on it, and bread. Jesus said to them, "Bring some of the fish that you have just caught." So Simon Peter went aboard and hauled the net ashore, full of large fish, a hundred fifty-three of them; and though there were so many, the net was not torn. Jesus said to them, "Come and have breakfast." . . .

When they had finished breakfast, Jesus said to Simon Peter, "Simon son of John, do you love me more than these?" He said to him, "Yes, Lord; you know that I love you." Jesus said to him, "Feed my lambs." A second time he said to him, "Simon son of John, do you love me?" He said to him, "Yes, Lord; you know that I love you." Jesus said to him, "Tend my sheep." He said to him the third time, "Simon son of John, do you love me?" Peter felt hurt because he said to him the third time, "Do you love me?" And he said to him, "Lord, you know everything; you know that I love you." Jesus said to him, "Feed my sheep." (John 21:4–12, 15–17)

Come and have breakfast.

Come and start again. Come because today is a new day, and God's mercies are new every morning.

When Peter sees that it is the Lord, he is so excited, he is beside himself. He throws himself off the boat and swims to shore. He just cannot wait to see Jesus.

"Forget the boat," he must be thinking, "Forget all those fish we just brought in, so many the net was strained. Forget my fishing companions. I need to see Jesus. Maybe, just maybe, things can come round right. Maybe there is healing for this broken place inside where I carry the jagged pieces of everything I have done wrong, everything that has gone wrong. Maybe, just maybe, the Lord will forgive me."

And he does.

Look in this story at what Jesus *doesn't* do. Jesus doesn't bring up the past to Peter. He doesn't say, "I told you so." He doesn't say, "I understand why you did what you did." He doesn't look backward. Instead he is in that exact moment. In that exact moment he asks Peter, "Do you love me?"

After having had lied three times to save his own skin, Peter now tells the truth three times to give his life to God. Right after breakfast. First thing in the day. He too arrives in that exact moment. Because now—right now—is the only time we can love.

When he hears Peter's declaration of commitment, Jesus just has one simple direction.

"Feed my lambs," Jesus tells him. Tend my lambs. Feed my sheep.

Christ the Good Shepherd enlists Peter—Peter the impetuous, Peter the bewildered, Peter the denier—to set the table of grace. To offer the hospitality and generosity of God to the world. To enable the emergence of a stable community in a benevolent and life-giving order[2]: by God's grace, the actual church. Us.

If God can use Peter, God can use me. If God can use Peter, God can use us.

We know God's intent for this world, and we know how far we have fallen. But our Lord is still inviting us to the breakfast table. Where Christ once offered us fish, a new economist is now offering us doughnuts. The doughnuts are metaphorical. But the metaphor is delicious.

Oxford economist Kate Raworth recently published *Doughnut Economics: Seven Ways to Think Like a Twenty-First-Century Economist.*[3] The discipline of economics is about the right ordering of our common home, our household together as a human society. Raworth opens her book by describing how the economic models we inherit from the nineteenth century fail us as we face today's challenges of inequity and climate change. They fail us, she says, because at their root is denial—a denial as profound as Peter's denial of Christ. Our leading economic models and policies, all the ways we have been taught to think about money and value, are predicated on two false concepts. The first is the concept that unlimited growth is possible, despite a limited planet. Second is the premise that as long as big corporations grow bigger, everybody will eventually get what they need. Both are based on denial.

Raworth says, "Today we have economies that need to grow, whether or not they make us thrive; what we need are economies that make us thrive, whether or not they grow."[4] Her response is to offer a different way of seeing our household together. She images it as a doughnut. The inner ring is the social foundation of human well-being wherein all have access to life's essentials such as food, education, and housing. The outer ring is an ecological ceiling, our planet's carrying capacity.

"Between these two sets of boundaries," she says, "lies a sweet spot—shaped unmistakably like a doughnut—that is both an ecologically safe and socially just space for humanity. The twenty-first-century task is an unprecedented one: to bring all of humanity into that safe and just space."[5]

This sounds like the intent that God has for us in Genesis: to create, from the primordial chaos, a stable community in a benevolent and life-giving order.[6] The truth is that every person inhabits a world that none of us created and on which all of us belong. This is God's world and God has created every soul upon the soil.

From the table of Abraham who offered hospitality in the wilderness, to the table of Christ who offers Peter a new beginning and a new commission by the lake, to our family tables and church altars, we continue the work of God creating and redeeming this world. We seek to continue that work. Every day I try and fail at it. Every day Christ invites me to begin again.

Come, he says, and have breakfast. Doughnuts and fish, bread and grape juice are on the menu. Denial about our current situation and the climates in which we live—ecological, spiritual, and political—is not holy nor is it welcome. Christ is truth and in him we have no fear (1 John 4:18). In him and by him we are fed to feed, to tend, to care. At his table we are renewed and sent to serve in his name. It's always time for breakfast.

CHAPTER FOUR

Taking Stewardship Seriously

One of the decorative pillows in our home came from my husband's late grandmother. It has a stained glass window design; on each side there is a saying. One side holds the famous prayer authored by Reinhold Niebuhr: "God grant me the serenity to accept the things I cannot change, the courage to change the things I can, and the wisdom to know the difference."

Since this prayer was first uttered in the 1930s, it has been written on paper, etched into metal and glass, cross-stitched, needlepointed, and even tattooed. For many, it summarizes a desire to find the peace of God through a combination of detachment (accepting what cannot be changed) and action (changing what can).

It's unfortunate that this prayer has been popularized under the name "Serenity Prayer," for the one who prays it asks God for much more than serenity. This is a prayer for wisdom: the capacity to discern, in a complex world, what can be changed and what cannot. It is also a prayer for bravery: the capacity to make change where it is possible. Only in situations where change is impossible is it a prayer for serenity, requesting a calm acceptance of what is beyond our capacity to control.

Here's the same prayer, reworded: "God grant me the wisdom to know what I can change, the courage to act for good despite my fears, and the serenity to accept what I can neither change nor influence." Is it the same prayer? Yes, it asks God for the same qualities. Is it a different prayer? Yes, it places the petitions in the opposite order. The revised prayer highlights our capacity for action. Serene acceptance of difficulty is not the first goal. It is a last resort. Serenity in the face of what cannot be changed is to be sought only in absolutely unalterable circumstances.

Much of the time, we *can* change something. That is especially true as it relates to the future of the church and the earth. Both can seem overwhelming. How can one person do something to shift an institution whose members number in the millions? How can one person do something to shift the rise of the planet's temperature? And yet, as data show an inexorable march toward numeric decline of the church and the warming of the planet, those of us who seek to proclaim Christ and tend Creation have a stark choice: move into unprecedented action or sink into unspeakable despair.

Neither the decline of the church's health nor the planet's is a matter for serenity, because neither is morally acceptable. In both cases our need is for action. We are called to change what we can change. Jesus taught us to pray, "Thy will be done on earth as it is in heaven." Who will reflect God's will on earth, if not God's servants in Jesus Christ? And what is more clearly the will of God than the renewal of God's people, the church, and the stewardship of God's Creation, the planet?

Alcoholics Anonymous, whose twelve-step program has saved countless lives, popularized Niehbur's words. One of the steps in AA can be adapted for our purposes. Step four calls for "a searching and fearless written moral inventory." Our roles as stewards call for a different kind of inventory: an inventory of what is within our capacity to control and/or to influence. What property do we steward? What resources are available to us for projects at the intersection of discipleship and care of Creation?

Stewardship through Inquiry and Action

In the summer of 2014, I was on the phone with Tom Perrin, a lay leader in the Diocese of Western Michigan who was raised in the congregation I then served. His church had just completed some outdoor trails and an altar for worship in their woods. I gave way to the sin of envy, and said, "That sounds wonderful. I wish we could do that too." Tom replied, "You *can* do this. You have just as much land as we do."

I was the associate priest; it had never occurred to me to consider the boundaries of our church property. I looked up the online property ownership map of our county and quickly realized that Tom was right. Our congregation was steward to almost four acres of God's Creation in the city of Grand Rapids. Much of it was wooded, perfect for a trail and altar project.

As one of the leaders of our youth ministry, I knew we had a couple potential future Eagle Scouts who would soon be seeking tangible projects to demonstrate leadership and contribute to the local community. We had an environmental educator in the congregation. I recognized the congregation's longstanding commitment to youth and a desire to see young people thrive. I was fairly sure that the lay leaders of the congregation would welcome an opportunity to use the church's property for that purpose.

It was not hard to create a program for the youth that year which included Bible study on the care of Creation. We involved future Eagle Scouts in thinking about options to serve their church through creating an outdoor place for prayer and worship.[1] With some shepherding through the vestry approval process, two different Eagle Scouts completed successive projects on church property. Today St. Andrew's has a trail in the woods, benches for contemplation, and an outdoor altar and cross. Even more important, St. Andrew's has been part of forming youth who "get" that the church has an essential role in caring for Creation. As the church themselves, they have put their own time, creativity, energy, and leadership into that goal.

None of that would have been possible without that simple inventory: what property does this church steward? Until Tom Perrin prompted me, I had not thought to ask that question. I thought that the church's property boundaries probably ended where the parking lot ended. It was the work of five minutes to discover the truth about our four acres. That quick inventory led to new investments by our youth in the life of the church and new investments by the congregation as well. Tangible projects for the care of Creation demonstrate to our church, our youth, and the wider community the importance of ecological stewardship in our life as disciples. They show we have the capacity to change. As the church created a place for worship in the woods and a young person handmade a cross to raise there, we fulfilled our core purpose as a church. We gave glory to God and tended Creation.

Although the inventory at St. Andrew's began with a question about our property boundaries, it also included our capacity as a congregation. St. Andrew's is not a particularly large church; approximately 125 people worship there each weekend. But it was a church that had a unique subset of rising Boy Scouts. Had we not recognized their presence as one of the church's assets, our Creation care project would have been impossible. Had they not been encouraged to see how they could provide their gifts in service to their faith community, they would have looked elsewhere for their final service project. Finally, the presence of an environmental educator in our congregation enabled our youth to have hands-on experience in a real place in Creation. As we studied the tracks made by creatures in the snow, our youth saw the evidence that many of God's creatures were at home on church land. They appreciated the chance to link the scriptural injunction that the Earth is the Lord's (Psalm 24) with the real property in their church's backyard.

Our year together with our Creation care program was relevant, accessible, and engaging to a younger generation. It began with very simple questions: What property do we steward? How can we learn to see it and treat it as God's Creation? How can we help others to experience it that way also?

A searching inventory and wise stewardship of church-owned assets is one thing; asking what we ourselves own as disciples takes the question to another level. As disciples, we must consider all that we are and all that we have as truly belonging to Christ. I know something about that journey from personal experience. At the same time I was working with St. Andrew's youth on the project in the church's woods, my cofounders and I were beginning Plainsong Farm.

Stewardship beyond the Comfort Zone

I had felt called to start a farm-based ministry since 2008, but didn't have the capacity to do so on my own. My husband and I, influenced by Wendell Berry, made our first home on a ten-acre property (a former organic farm) in 2001—but neither of us were farmers. I figured that out as I started gardens and tended chickens, trying to be faithful to God's call to me. I thought I needed to make a farm first, before starting a farm-based ministry. But I quickly discovered that I was a failure at tending land, animals, and plants; God had made me to tend faith communities. My chickens survived, but weeds overtook my gardens. I found joy in my priestly vocation; I did not find delight in farming. My results in each vocation also indicated that my time was more fruitful tending souls than soil. I lamented that fact; my values are aligned with care for the earth, and I regretted how poorly I did so personally.

The day came that I confessed my failures to God and asked God to take over (more on that story in chapter six). I realized that farmers needed to live in my house and tend our ten acres if the farm-based ministry God had called me to create would ever actually begin. Through a combination of providence and privilege, my family was able to move to another house. Then I began the (terrifying) process of finding farmers who would move into our house, tend our property, and work with me on bringing God's dream to life.

I met Mike and Bethany Edwardson through mutual friends. It was clear early on that they were the right people to embark on the crazy adventure of start-up farm-based ministry. Like me, they felt called to start a farm-based ministry. When they had outlined their goals together early in their married life, "Have a farm connected to the church" was at the top. Having begun gardens at their home, their church, and their school, they knew how to tend the land. They were smart, thoughtful, caring people who were highly motivated to begin a farm ministry too.

We knew the entire concept of farm-based ministry was new. None of us expected funding or institutional support from any church until we had at least one (hopefully successful) growing season behind us. Mike and Bethany were recent graduates of college (Bethany) and college plus seminary (Mike). They were more than willing to work and I trusted them with our property. But they had no funds to contribute to the project. Mike thought we could start up a small farm on fifteen thousand dollars. He brought a budget to show his plans. I took a deep breath, prayed some more, and talked with my husband. We had fifteen thousand dollars. We contributed it to the project, without knowing if it would ever return to us.

For a part-time pastor and a firefighter, fifteen thousand dollars is a lot of money. It was a scary decision, but it was even more frightening to imagine not fulfilling what I felt God was calling me to do.

Remember that rephrased Serenity Prayer? "God grant me the wisdom to know what I can change, the courage to act for good despite my fears, and the serenity to accept what I can neither change nor influence." A moment came when I realized that I finally could begin Plainsong Farm after almost seven years of waiting, hoping, praying, and failing. The Edwardsons wanted to take on the farming side and our family owned the property outright. For a few years we had been both highly frugal and highly compensated; we could provide capital to the project. Suddenly "start a farm ministry" went from "I need serenity to accept the fact that this is impossible" to "this is possible, but I need courage to take one more step."

I began to do many things I had never done before: hire a lawyer, hire an accountant, set up a new entity, and entrust my family's property to another family. Every day was frightening, because there was so much risk involved. What if I didn't know what I was doing (which I didn't) and I did it wrong? What if the Edwardsons turned out to be terrible partners or terrible farmers? What if my family's house was destroyed?

The project with the youth in the woods at St. Andrew's and the start-up of the farm ministry occurred at the same time. One was just slightly outside my comfort zone (St. Andrew's) and the other was wholly and completely outside my comfort zone (Plainsong Farm). At St. Andrew's, I knew how to work with youth and how to develop new programs. The congregation had existed for over fifty years, I had worked there for over five, and the trust level of the church was high. The work was well within my capacity. If it failed, it wouldn't take the whole church down. Everyone would understand and move on. But at Plainsong Farm, none of that was true. I didn't know how to start a farm or a farm-based ministry. I didn't know what programs we would be starting, but knew the earliest stages of any new venture were critically important to its future culture. If the partnership failed or the farm failed, I wasn't sure I would give the time and funding again; every aspect of start-up had a "now or never" feeling. (No pressure.) Mike, Bethany, and I barely knew each other and were still building trust amongst ourselves. Creating a new farm-based ministry seemed to be within our capacity. However, this was my family's home, property, and capital. The level of risk felt incredibly high.

Stewardship and Risk

When I read the Gospels, I can see that Jesus expects us to embrace risk as part of our life of discipleship. He makes that clear in the parable of the talents:

> For it is as if a man, going on a journey, summoned his slaves and entrusted his property to them; to one he gave five talents, to another two, to another one, to each according to his ability. Then he went away. The one who had received the five talents went off at once and traded with them, and made five more talents. In the same way, the one who had the two talents made two more talents. But the one who had received the one talent went off and dug a hole in the ground and hid his master's money. After a long time the master of those slaves came and settled accounts with them. Then the one who had received the five talents came forward, bringing five more talents, saying, "Master, you handed over to me five talents; see, I have made five more talents." His master said to him, "Well done, good and trustworthy slave; you have been trustworthy in a few things, I will put you in charge of many things; enter into the joy of your master." And the one with the two talents also came forward, saying, "Master, you handed over to me two talents; see, I have made two more talents." His master said to him, "Well done, good and trustworthy slave; you have been trustworthy in a few

things, I will put you in charge of many things; enter into the joy of your master." Then the one who had received the one talent also came forward, saying, "Master, I knew that you were a harsh man, reaping where you did not sow, and gathering where you did not scatter seed; so I was afraid, and I went and hid your talent in the ground. Here you have what is yours." But his master replied, "You wicked and lazy slave! You knew, did you, that I reap where I did not sow, and gather where I did not scatter? Then you ought to have invested my money with the bankers, and on my return I would have received what was my own with interest. So take the talent from him, and give it to the one with the ten talents. For to all those who have, more will be given, and they will have an abundance; but from those who have nothing, even what they have will be taken away. As for this worthless slave, throw him into the outer darkness, where there will be weeping and gnashing of teeth." (Matt. 25:14–30)

The master leaves for a long journey and entrusts his money to his slaves. Knowing that they have different abilities, the master gives them different amounts. These are no small sums. If this story were taking place today, the master would say to his slaves, "Here's five million dollars for you, two million dollars for you, and a million dollars for you. Take care of it for me until I return." Jesus's hearers would have been absolutely staggered by the amount of money involved. The entire story is founded on risk: the master takes a risk, leaving his home and his fortune in the hands of others. The first two slaves take risks, taking the money to the marketplace and trading with it. But the third slave is too afraid to risk. He does what was common at the time: he buries the money in the ground for safekeeping.

A long time passes. Finally the master returns. And when he does, he demands an accounting from his slaves. The first two, who risked actively trading, have doubled the money. The master is pleased, and they receive promotions. The last slave, who buried the money instead of taking the risk of loss and gain, is called wicked and lazy, and thrown into the outer darkness. He wanted to protect himself, to play it safe, to be sure he could return what he had been given. But his very instinct to play it safe was his undoing. Ironically, he receives his master's disapproval exactly because he acts out of fear of his master's displeasure.[2]

Jesus tells this story as part of a larger set of lessons about his second coming: be ready at any time for my return, but do not wait for me passively. We aren't meant to hoard or bury the gifts we have been given. We are meant to take them out into the world so that they can bear fruit and multiply for the kingdom. As Jesus says elsewhere, "From everyone to whom much has been given, much will be required; and from the one to whom much has been entrusted, even more will be demanded" (Luke 12:48).

That's why the Serenity Prayer, in any version, includes a request for wisdom. It takes wisdom to discern our gifts. It takes wisdom to see what is within our capacity to change. And it takes wisdom to recognize that sometimes the risk of inaction is greater than the risk of action—even when the risk of action is great.

As we were beginning Plainsong Farm, day after day I did things I had never done before. They scared me. I kept at it as the necessary and important work of David Hurst's learning loop (see pages 21–24). Get up every day without knowing what you are doing, and do something anyway, without knowing if it is the right thing or if you are doing it in the right way. I knew that the necessary work of discipleship was to take what I had (a house, ten acres, and fifteen thousand dollars) and offer it for the work of God in the world. It was a small thing in comparison with what the saints of the church had offered in their time.

I didn't want to be the servant who hoarded out of fear; I wanted to be the servant who put what I had in trust to work for the greater glory of God. I wanted to change the things I could, beginning with me. I couldn't alter everything, but I could change something. I could shift what I was doing each day to include something new. I did that for enough days in a row, with enough of the right people, and got enough right (although certainly not everything), that Plainsong Farm became real. People are fed in both body and soul through the work of the farm. That is entirely due to the grace and providence of God, who welcomed me into the body of Christ in my baptism and empowered me with the Holy Spirit to be an agent of grace in the world. It was due to Mike and Bethany Edwardson and the donors, volunteers, neighbors, members, and partners who have enabled our story to take shape.

Maybe you don't have ten acres and fifteen thousand dollars. Maybe your church doesn't have land in the woods. But every person has been entrusted with something incredibly valuable: the breath in your lungs, the gift of your life, and the treasure of each day. We are also entrusted with the gospel of life, death, and resurrection of Jesus Christ. Not only are we alive today, we have been incorporated into the body of Christ, which lives forever. We have received teachings, rituals, songs, and stories: truth to guide our lives. The gift of life and the gift of faith are priceless.

Serving the world in Christ's name is risky. But it yields a rich reward, here and now and in the life to come. As disciples, we are servants of a master who risked everything, and so doing, redeemed the world. We follow in his footsteps when we also embrace risk for the sake of redemption. We may wonder at our sanity sometimes (I know I did). But as the planet warms and the church's numbers decline, it is madness to think that we can stay in our comfort zones. There is too much within our capacity to change.

The Daughters of the King, a lay order for Episcopal women, repeat this prayer at each of their gatherings:

For His Sake . . . I am but one, but I am one.
I cannot do everything, but I can do something.
What I can do, I ought to do.
What I ought to do, by the grace of God I will do.
Lord, what will you have me do?[3]

INTERLUDE
MEETING MILLENNIALS IN GARDENS AND FIELDS

When I read Wendell Berry in the late 1990s, I realized my food choices had a direct impact on the health of my local community and the planet as a whole. I wanted to share what I knew about food miles, sustainability, and health with the congregation I then served and I was willing to go out on a limb to do so. I preached my first sermon on the connections between food and faith in 2002. Around the same time, I began to go to food and farm gatherings. I was never a farmer, but I was interested in how farming fit into our common future.

When I preached that sermon I was thirty-one years old. I noticed that most of the people in the church I served were older than I was. I thought it was temporary. After all, I was still a fairly young adult. And at the turn of the millennium, it wasn't yet evident that America was at the cusp of a long-term trend in disengagement from organized religion. Like almost everyone else, I expected those in their twenties would come back to church someday soon. I thought teens being raised in the church would find the practice of faith just as meaningful as I did. I was wrong.

We all know better now. The Pew Center reported in 2015, "As the Millennial generation enters adulthood, its members display much lower levels of religious affiliation, including less connection with Christian churches, than older generations. Fully 36% of young

Millennials (those between the ages of 18 and 24) are religiously unaffiliated, as are 34% of older Millennials (ages 25–33)."[1]

In many churches, nobody needs a Pew Center report to state what is evident: most people under forty aren't coming through the doors. And it's not just your church. The Episcopal Church's internal reporting recently showed that "31% of Episcopal church members are age 65 and older, as compared to only 14% of the American public. By contrast, 26% of Americans are age 19 or younger, as compared to only 16% of Episcopalians."[2] The overall age structure of the Episcopal Church does not reflect the general United States population, as the following chart makes clear:

Population of the USA and Episcopal Church by Age (2014)[3]

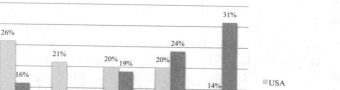

I'm in that "median adults" group, right in the middle of the chart. From that viewpoint I noticed something important: even as I stayed a "young person" in an aging church, I also became an "old person" in a completely different context.

From 2002 to 2017 I actively participated in two different communities: the church and the wider food movement. Over those fifteen years I noticed something important: while the church kept getting older, the food movement kept getting younger. As I moved through my thirties and into my forties, I remained the youngest person at many clergy gatherings. At the same time, I became one of the older people at food and farm gatherings.

In 2014, the same year the Episcopal Church reported the disturbing demographic information charted above, the National Gardening Association did a report of its own. *Garden to Table: A Five-Year Look at Food Gardening in America* stated:

> In 2008 there were 8 million Millennial food gardeners and in 2013 there were 13 million, an increase of 63%. In 2008 Millennials spent a total of $632 million on food gardening, and in 2013 they spent a total of $1.192 billion, an increase of 89%. . . . The largest increase in the number of food gardeners by age from 2008 to 2013 were households aged 18–34.[4]

It is painting with too broad a brush to suggest that the Millennial generation is skipping church to stay home and grow food. However, one thing is sure: the Millennial generation is less engaged in church and more engaged in gardening.

The logic behind this trend is clear. The early 2000s brought to light massive scandals and ushered in massive conflicts in the life of the church, making organized Christianity less trustworthy as a repository of hopes and values. Meanwhile, the combination of 9/11 and the stock market crash of 2008 sent shock waves through a generation that learned at a young age and firsthand about both our country's vulnerability and lack of economic stability. At the same time, the scientific consensus about climate change became clear—and the church largely stayed silent about the largest crisis of our day. Finally, critical thinking about the industrial food system reached a new level with the publication of *Animal, Vegetable, Miracle* (2007) and *The Omnivore's*

Dilemma (2009), and the release of *Food, Inc.* (2009). As the concept of "food miles" took hold and Michelle Obama planted a garden at the White House, growing your own food was a practical way to improve your health, bolster your economic resilience, decrease greenhouse gases, and discover the wonder of life in soil and seed.

Simply putting in a church garden doesn't mean that Millennials will show up at your door. As the food movement took hold across America, many churches began or renewed community garden ministries. These were largely seen as outreach ministries providing access to healthy food to those who could not otherwise afford it: the work of food justice or food sovereignty. Most simply grew food without growing new Christians or reengaging young people questioning the relevance of the church. Despite our many active food ministries, and despite the many ways Holy Scripture reflects an agricultural worldview, the church is just beginning to learn how to create and renew relationships with God in gardens, fields, and kitchens.

To reach a generation that largely gave up on church—for good reasons—will take many one-on-one relationships with trustworthy and authentic disciples. These relationships could start in kitchens, gardens, and fields, working together by cooking, weeding, and tending. It is only through relationship that we—the continuing church—might begin to listen to what turned people away from church. Through relationships we can demonstrate the love of God in Christ. We can share our stories of how our lives have been changed by knowing and serving Christ in the church. Relationships can begin weeding a church garden or cooking a community lunch. Mutually respectful relationships where active churchgoers *listen* as much as talk are the only way we can, one by one, invite people to reconsider being church together.

The core stories of the Christian faith center around a garden (Eden), land (Israel/Palestine), and table (Holy Eucharist). It is natural and logical for us to meet people in a garden, on a field, and at a table. The data indicates that a younger generation may be more willing to listen to the gospel in those settings. Jesus told stories about weeds and wheat, soil and seeds, vines and branches, sheep and shepherd. His last earthly ministry was to provide us a meal through which to remember him, a meal in which he is still and always present until he comes again. Inviting people to meet Jesus in gardens, on land, and at tables may be exactly the way to help a younger generation rediscover his ministry—and continue to learn from him ourselves.

CHAPTER FIVE

Neighbors Together

I n the early 1970s, Willie James Jennings was an African-American youth in Grand Rapids, Michigan. He tells the story of an incident from his late childhood that stayed with him for over four decades in the first few pages of his excellent book *The Christian Imagination: Theology and the Origins of Race* (Yale University, 2010). If it had happened to me as it happened to him, I would remember it too.

He and his mother heard footsteps approach as they were working in their family garden. Two white men drew near and introduced themselves as being "from First Christian Reformed Church down the street." They asked his mother's name, but that was all they asked. They then proceeded to inform her of the ministries of their church. The older man talked about the activities for children, what they were hoping to do in the neighborhood, and much more. It seemed to Jennings that this was a prepared speech. The younger man bent down and asked Jennings how old he was, where he went to school, and if he liked his school. Both men struck him as utterly lost. As Jennings writes:

> The strangeness of this event lay not only in their appearance in our backyard but also in the obliviousness of these men as to whom they were addressing—Mary Jennings, one of the pillars of New Hope Missionary Baptist Church. I thought it incredibly odd that they never once asked her if she went to church, if she was a Christian, or even if she believed in God. Mary and her twin sister, Martha,

were about as close to their scriptural counterparts as you could get. Without fail they were in their customary seats every Sunday, and you could calibrate almost every activity of the church by and around them or us, their children. In addition, every Sunday they would visit every single person on the sick and shut-in list. The depth and complexities of Mary's faith were unfathomable, as unfathomable as the blindness of these men to our Christian lives. . . . I remember this event because it underscored an inexplicable strangeness embedded in the Christianity I lived and observed. Experiences like these field a question that has grown in hermeneutic force for me: Why did they not know us? They should have known us very well.[1]

As Jennings continues the story, he makes clear that one of his favorite places to be in the world as a twelve-year-old boy was the parking lot of the First Christian Reformed Church. It had the best basketball court around, and was only two hundred yards from his house. He was there often. And yet, regardless of the relationship he already had with their congregation, neighbors from the church where he spent time each and every week came to his door as if he were a lost stranger and they were missionaries seeking to save his soul.

Neighborliness Gone Wrong

Grand Rapids, Michigan, is my adopted hometown, which means I know the place of Jennings's narrative. I came into John Calvin's territory when I moved here. The Reformation theologian has an outsize influence on this region. Calvin College is here, as are the headquarters of both the Reformed Church in America and the Christian Reformed Church, cousin denominations. "If you ain't Dutch, you ain't much" is a Grand Rapids tongue-in-cheek saying.

First Christian Reformed Church, which sent the two men to Jennings's home, was one of the founding congregations of our community. The cornerstone for the building outside of which Jennings played basketball was laid in 1911.[2] When the congregation decided to build at the corner of Bates and Henry, the southeast side of this city was primarily white. The Great Migration of African-Americans fleeing the Jim Crow South changed that. As Southern African-Americans came to Grand Rapids, an unwelcoming white community confined them to the southeast side of the city. African-Americans settled in the neighborhood around First Christian Reformed Church. White families moved out of their houses as Black families moved in.

It takes just two minutes to walk from Jennings's house to the basketball court at First Christian Reformed Church. Jennings's family and the congregation of First Christian Reformed were neighbors to one another. They were disciples of Jesus together. And yet they did not even know each others' names, much less how God was at work in their lives. Worse, when the members of First Christian Reformed went to visit Jennings's family, they implied by their words and their actions that this African-American family was in need of virtuous white people in order to come to know, love, and serve God. Clearly that was not the case.

Inspired in part by his question in the garden that afternoon, Jennings grew up to be a theologian and professor of systematic theology at Yale Divinity School. His undergraduate degree is from Calvin College. His book is required reading in seminaries. Every time anyone opens it for the first time, they read a story about Christian neighborliness gone wrong—in my hometown.

It didn't have to be that way. When Jesus told us "love your neighbor as yourself," he surely did not intend for strangers to deliver speeches about the virtues of their ministries. That is not how love acts. Paul reminds us:

Love is patient; love is kind; love is not envious or boastful or arrogant or rude. It does not insist on its own way; it is not irritable or resentful; it does not rejoice in wrongdoing, but rejoices in the truth. It bears all things, believes all things, hopes all things, endures all things. (1 Cor. 13:4–7)

It is hard to love a stranger. It is certain that the way to love does not begin by describing the programs of a congregation. And yet I am confident that the two men from First Christian Reformed Church are not the only Christians who have taken this approach to ministering in the neighborhood.

My twenty years' experience in congregational ministry has largely been that when we engage in the neighborhood, we have a hidden agenda: we want the neighbors to attend our church. I am guilty of this tendency myself. It springs from the fact that I love my church. There, I have found a community and a home there that helps God grow me. I want others to have that experience too, to be blessed as I have been blessed. As much as I am made uncomfortable by Jennings's description of his interaction with the gentlemen from First Reformed, I can also see myself in them. The mistake they made is one I could easily have made myself.

A Question, Not an Answer

Contrast the encounter of Willie James Jennings and the ambassadors from First Christian Reformed with Frank Logue's experience planting King of Peace Episcopal Church in Kingsland, Georgia. A new priest, he was sent by his bishop to begin a church in a community that was growing near a submarine base. He could have begun in any number of ways. He began by knocking on doors and talking with strangers. With anyone who was willing to talk with him, he said this: "I'm starting a church, but I'm not here to ask you to come to the church. I'm here because the church I'm starting will make a positive difference for the whole community. What·do you think this community most needs that this new church could provide?"[3]

Instead of beginning with a speech about the church, he began with a question. It was a question that anyone could answer, because it drew on knowledge and experience they already had. They were asked to reflect, as neighbors together, on their neighborhood. As neighbors together they could try to discern what God was seeking to bring to life in their midst.

It is no coincidence that Willie James Jennings's story about being visited by two white men is the beginning of a theological book about the development of the concept of racial identity and the displacement of native peoples. It is no coincidence that Frank Logue's story about asking questions of his neighbors is the beginning of a thriving congregation that continues to serve its community today. And it is no coincidence that I open this chapter with both of these stories. One is a cautionary tale, and the other is a good example.

In my area, the established churches are the Reformed Church and the Roman Catholic Church. The Episcopal Church is tiny in comparison to each. But in some places, the established church— the church with paid staff, an organized life together, abundant endowed funds, multiple facilities, both secular ministries and worshipping communities—is the Episcopal Church. Even where we are relatively small and few (much of Michigan, for example), we carry with us the establishment mentality that is part of our Church of England heritage. This heritage is both blessing and curse. It is a blessing because we inherit a practice of faith that teaches us that our role in the community is to care for the health of the whole. It is a curse because we inherit a practice of faith that teaches us to believe we have a right to be here, and a right to set the terms of engagement with others. Establishment can too easily lead to an attitude of entitlement. And entitlement is the opposite of love—of both God and neighbor.

To Paul's beautiful description of love in 1 Corinthians 13, I would add a few lines: love is curious. Love wants to learn more. Love is engaged in ongoing relationship. And as Christ calls us to love our neighbors as ourselves, an attitude of curiosity is the place to begin. We are not the only people working to steward Creation and benefit our community. Whatever initiative God seeks to bring to life through us joins a plethora of other projects that God is also calling to life through others.

Food and Faith

Among the key neighbors from whom I seek to learn and through whom I see the work of God is the Jewish organization Hazon (*www.hazon.org*). Founded in 1999, Hazon describes itself this way: "We create healthier and more sustainable communities in the Jewish world and beyond." Founder Nigel Savage says, "[E]verything the organization has done, one way or another, involves pointing the Jewish community or the Jewish tradition outwards to try and take on some of the most important issues of our time."[4]

Hazon's initiatives include a farm that grows young adult leaders along with good food, free curricula and resources for congregations, the largest faith-based community supported agriculture network in the country, and much more. Their goal—healthier and more sustainable communities in their faith tradition and beyond—is easy to embrace. I am a witness that they are achieving the "beyond" part of their mission, because Hazon has been a model for me, demonstrating ways to cultivate healthier and more sustainable communities in the Episcopal world and beyond.

I discovered Hazon's Adamah Farm, a young adult program, in Fred Bahnson's book *Soil and Sacrament* (Simon & Schuster, 2013). Bahnson's description makes it clear that Adamah's program was designed by someone who understands that the ecological crisis is a crisis of religion. Adamah enables young adults to serve three-month fellowships incorporating the study and practice of Judaism and the study and practice of sustainable agriculture. Young adults are invited to engage deeply and simultaneously in the work of religious renewal and the work of healing Creation.

Informed by the Jewish practice of *kashrut*, Hazon places food at the center of their work on faith, health, and sustainability. The organization reflects an essential reality: everybody eats, every single day, multiple times a day. Every single person can relate to the necessity of food for survival. Food was essential long before money even existed. And food plays an incredibly important part in the stories of Holy Scripture.

Life begins in a garden with low-hanging fruit. Expelled from the garden after trespassing against God's boundaries, Adam is reminded that he is a creature of the earth that will now work hard for food (Gen. 3). The people of Israel leave for Egypt because there is a famine in the land; they are able to return because God provides manna in the wilderness for their journey. The prophet Isaiah, envisioning God's full and final rule, describes it as a mountaintop feast for all peoples (Isa. 25). All of these scriptures, along with the prohibition against cooking a kid (goat) in its mother's milk (Exodus and Deuteronomy) informed Hazon's approach to food. As their website explains, "For 3,000 years, Judaism has been encouraging us to think critically about the food we eat, the land our food comes from, and the ways our food choices affect the health of our community and our planet."[5]

The importance of food is just as evident in the Christian faith. When God comes to us in Christ, his feeding miracles are one of the ways his divinity is made known. And the last gift he offers to us in his earthly ministry is not a set of tablets etched in stone, but a memorial meal in which we—along with Christians throughout the ages—receive Christ Himself. That meal is meant to inspire all our meals.

"Eating is an agricultural act," states Wendell Berry.[6] I would add: Eating is a theological act. Now that most of us no longer eat by the sweat of our own brow (Gen. 3) but by an industrial system dependent on the labor of others, we no longer see the immediate implications of our food choices. But studies show our current food system, including feed, fertilizer, and pesticide manufacture, processing, transportation, refrigeration and waste disposal, accounts for 30 percent or more of total annual global greenhouse gas emissions.[7] Therefore, the way we eat has an impact on the health of Creation. The study, which cites the climate impact of our current food system, also points toward a better way: the sequestration of carbon through regenerative agriculture. The Rodale Institute states,

> We have proven that organic agriculture and, specifically, regenerative organic agriculture can sequester carbon from the atmosphere and reverse climate change. . . . With the use of cover crops, compost, crop rotation and reduced tillage, we can actually sequester more carbon than is currently emitted, tipping the needle past 100% to reverse climate change. We know that agriculture has played a role in creating climate chaos but, now, with your help, it can be part of the solution.[8]

Scripture makes clear that human beings are essentially one with the substance of the earth. Science makes clear that if we tend the soil well, life can flourish on this garden planet. Because eating is an agricultural act, the way we eat shapes the way farmers farm. We can express love of neighbor through our individual food choices and advocacy for good farm and food policies. Farmers are our rural neighbors, and farmers' lives are directly impacted by the way we eat. A report from the Pew Commission on Industrial Food Animal Production states:

> The industrialization of American agriculture has transformed the character of agriculture itself and, in so doing, the face of rural America. The family-owned farm producing a diverse mix of crops and food animals is largely gone as an economic entity, replaced by ever-larger industrial farms producing just one animal species or growing just one crop, and rural communities have fared poorly. Industrialization has been accompanied by increasing farm size and gross farm sales, lower family income, higher poverty rates, lower retail sales, lower housing quality, and lower wages for farm workers.[9]

It is time for the Christian community to ask some questions. Has our acceptance of all food as "clean" (Acts 10) become a stumbling block to those who wonder how we can claim to follow Jesus while eating food that causes harm to Creation? Are we eating food that has been offered to the idol of money, that which Jesus said we could not serve along with God (Matt. 6:24)? If we are, how can we bring our food practices more into alignment with our faith?

Our family began to source our meat from Jeff and Karen Lubbers when we first moved to Grand Rapids. They kept a small farm and raised their animals on pasture. It was healthier for the animals, for us, and for the soil. More than once I heard Karen say, "The best thing is to grow your own food. The second best thing is to know the farmer who does." When we know our farmer, we know the practices that grow our food. We know our food dollars go directly to people making a living from the land. We get to know some of our neighbors. We know our place, which is tended by these farmers day in and day out, throughout the seasons. And we know we are making a difference.

My husband and I began to purchase food directly from farmers on our own. How much impact would we have had if we had done so as part of a congregation? Hazon began its direct-purchasing program for Jewish congregations in 2004. By 2016, there were 10,000 Jewish people putting 2 million dollars into more than fifty local farms. Nigel Savage said:

> On the one hand it's putting Jewish purchasing power behind local organic farms. That is one small good. Secondly it lets you and your family gets local organic produce and at a fair price. Thirdly, it enables us to reframe Jewish life so that people go to synagogue or JCC not just to go to services on Friday or Saturday, but also to meet their farmer and their neighbors on a Wednesday. Fourthly, if people don't pick up their produce, we give it to people in need. Our CSA gave at least 40,000 pounds of produce to people in need last year.[10]

Food is what we have in common, with one another and with humanity across all generations. We always had to eat in the past; we will always have to eat in the future. The way we eat makes a difference to our neighbors as well as ourselves, now and for the foreseeable future. We can choose a way of eating that creates healthier and more sustainable communities by knowing our farmers. We can do what Willie James Jennings's mother was doing that day when the two men from the First Christian Reformed Church walked into her yard. Why was she outside, ready to be a neighbor? She was growing food for her family in her garden.

How would their interaction have been different if, instead of telling her all about their church programs, they had begun by saying, "We go to church around the corner. As disciples of Jesus, we want to know and love our neighbors. We thought we'd start by saying hello. Your garden looks beautiful. Would you mind taking a minute to tell us about what you grow?"

INTERLUDE
FINDING THE CHRISTIAN FOOD MOVEMENT

Hazon coined the term "Jewish food movement." Founder Nigel Savage needed an umbrella term for work helping Jewish congregations engage with sustainable food initiatives based on the ethics of eating passed down through his tradition. In 2007, a group of leaders drafted goals for a Jewish food movement to seek to achieve over the coming seven years—a sabbatical cycle that is an ancient part of Jewish tradition. In early 2014, as Savage was reflecting on the outcomes of that effort, he said, "I went into Google this afternoon, and in quote marks I typed 'Catholic Food Movement,' and there was one hit. I typed 'Christian Food Movement,' and there were two hits. I typed 'Jewish Food Movement,' and there were 81,300 hits."[1]

Reading Nigel Savage's words about a Christian food movement later that year, I thought to myself, "I know that can't be right."

In one way, Nigel was completely correct. In 2014, there was absolutely no organized or identifiable Christian food movement. But because I had been baffled by this call from God to start a farm ministry for a while, I had a sharp eye out for Christian work at the intersection of food and faith. By 2014, I knew multiple Christian farms, organizations, and even a few experimental faith communities that integrated the practice of discipleship with sustainable agriculture. I decided to make a list of what I knew, and share it with the world. After all, I reasoned, I already had a blog. How hard could it be?

I learned something important as I created a list drawing together the organizations and people that I then knew. The Christian food movement was not well organized. It was not self-aware. But it definitely existed and was undergirded by strong theological foundations. Christians see the earth—from which all food comes—as God's good Creation. Christians realize that a sacred meal—Holy Communion—is one of our faith's central practices. Christians know that food is a gift from God for which we give thanks.

Disciples put faith into practice in a variety of ways. Some tend land as farmers and gardeners seeking to steward soil. Some feed hungry people as gleaners and growers. Some advocate for wiser policy choices. Some work in interfaith coalitions to shift local food systems. Some reflect and write on the meaning of food and faith. Some simply choose to grow and cook real food and share it. When all this work is gathered in one place, it adds up to something big: a Christian food movement.

Early in 2015, I categorized the books, farms, and resources I found and made a PDF document listing them all. I made it available as a free download on my blog. Three hundred people downloaded it, far more than I imagined would be interested. Some sent me more organizations and individuals to include. Others wrote me letters thanking me profusely for my work. As a mainline clergyperson, I was most astonished by the fact that people under the age of thirty-five started spontaneously contacting me to ask for help navigating their faith and food context. It was evident that even though this was unfunded work, it was necessary work. At the end of 2015, with the help of volunteers Abby Bok and Erin Skidmore, I released the second version of the guide with additions that had been suggested for inclusion. I couldn't help but notice that both Abby and Erin were members of the Millennial generation—and this project inspired them to volunteer hours of their time.

When I e-mailed the second guide to everyone that had downloaded the first version, I included a request for a small amount of funding to pay the direct costs of building a website to hold the guide and make it more easily accessible. One e-mail yielded the funding I requested. The website (*www.christianfoodmovement.org*) was completed in late 2016. The directory grew exponentially in just the two years since I began the first version. There were now not only multiple dinner churches to include, but also farm churches and garden churches. There was faith-based urban agriculture and overseas sustainable agriculture missions training. There was an explosion of books. Many listings were of projects and programs that hadn't even existed two years earlier.

I started the guide because I was hungry for information. Now I keep it because the people who are part of this movement provide me inspiration. They write in with their stories: Josh Payne, a thirty-something farmer who tends six hundred acres with his eighty-eight-year-old grandfather. Inspired by his Christian faith, he's navigating the challenge of converting the farm to regenerative agriculture to mitigate climate change while also making a living for his family.[2] Kendall Vanderslice, the twentysomething dinner church researcher and writer whose post "Dinner Churches Spring Up Nationwide" was shared thousands of times on Facebook within the first few months of the Christian food movement site's existence.[3] The Rev. Derrick Weston, a Presbyterian pastor, wrote: "I believe that it is time for the church to see food as its number one issue, the issue that cuts across race, gender, sexual orientation, and politics and is so often deeply connected to all of them. In my days as a pastor I would regularly invite people to come and feast at the Lord's Table. It is time to make that invitation real, tangible, and personal. It is time for the church to say to the world: 'Come! The table is ready!'"[4]

Everybody eats. No matter who you are or where you live, food is relevant to your life. The home page on the Christian food movement website says it all:

When we eat, we acknowledge our complete dependence on God. We recognize our mutual dependence with all Creation. We didn't create the seeds or the soil or the beasts of the field. They are God's handiwork. And so are we. *Every human soul.*

God uses food to remind us that—though we are made in the image of God—we are not God. We say grace before meals to help us remember: We are the Creation, not the Creator. We are dust, and to dust we shall return; God only is immortal. Our role is to glorify God with our days—to glorify God with our work, with our rest, with our worship. With our meals.

As Christ's disciples, we practice what He taught us.

We remember the loaves and fish that fed the multitude, and we seek good food for all. We remember the parable of the weeds and the wheat, and we seek lives that bear fruit for God's reign. We remember that through Him all things were made. We seek ways to live wisely on the good earth, so that generations yet to come may still give Him thanks for their lives.

Welcome to the Christian food movement.

The wider food movement has grown into a significant force in policy and culture over the past two decades. Christians have been quietly participating all along. But as more new ministries incorporating food and agriculture begin, the need has become urgent for us to find one another.

We need to learn from each other. We need to pray for each other. We need to listen together for what God would have us do.

That's the purpose of this site. It is dedicated to the glory of God and the welfare of God's Creation.

In the name of Christ who said, "I was a stranger, and you welcomed me," you are invited to enter in.[5]

CHAPTER SIX

Pray, Then Plan

Harvard Divinity School held a worship service to send off their field education students into their student ministry positions for the first time in 1993. Usually the school offered multiple worship services each week: one for the Episcopalians, one for the Unitarian Universalists, and one called simply "Community Worship." Other services of worship came and went depending upon who requested the use of the chapel.

A first-year student went to the field education supervisor and asked if it would be possible for one of the early fall community worship services to center on blessing the seminarians before we began our work in the community. The request was granted, and a small planning team was put together. I served on that planning team. I was twenty-two years old and had attended church for the first time only three years before. I didn't have much to offer. I offered a reading from the poet Marvin Bell.

Marvin Bell had come to my college campus when I was a senior. In preparation for that visit, I had read one of his essays in the *American Poetry Review*. In those days I was struggling with the questions that all college seniors face: Who am I becoming? What future do I seek? Bell, with his rumpled persona and down-to-earth speaking and writing style, cut through everyone's pretensions. His essay was ostensibly about an approach to poetry, but it was really an approach to life. It offered a choice and a challenge: were you seeking a way of life, or were you building a career? Bell wrote:

Poetry is a way of life, not a career. A career means you solicit the powerful and the famous. A way of life means you live where you are with the people around you. A career means you become an authority. A way of life means you stay a student, even if you teach for a living. A career means your life increasingly comes from your art. A way of life means your art continues to arise from your life. Careerism feeds on the theoretical, the fancified, the complicated, the coded, and the overwrought: all forms of psychological coward-ice. A way of life is nourished by the practical, the unadorned, the complex, and a direct approach to the mysterious.[1]

When those words were read in the chapel of Harvard Divinity School in September of 1993, we took the liberty of swapping in "ministry" for "poetry" in the first line, believing the main point still applied.

The congregation that Wednesday noon was a full house. A sig-nificant percentage of the student body responded to the opportunity to pray together in common worship before going out into our field education sites. We wanted to be blessed by our instructors who some-how were willing to take a risk on us. We wanted as much wisdom as we could soak up. We were about to begin our very first experiences in ministry. If we made mistakes—and we were sure to make mistakes—we could hurt real people. We were beginning the daunting process of speaking for God. We were appropriately terrified and knew we needed to pray. We also needed to hear that—despite appearances—we were not beginning professional preparation for a career. We were embracing a way of life.

Ministry is a way of life for all Christians. This is the vow we make in baptism. Every day, disciples of Jesus Christ go out into the world the same way we students went out into our field education sites. We go out certain that we do not, in and of ourselves, have the capacity to meet the world's needs. We go out not knowing what will happen next. We go out because we are *sent* out: sent to proclaim the gospel of the love of God in Christ Jesus our Lord. Although some make that a career, it is fundamentally a way of life. "I am the way, the truth, and the life," said Jesus (John 14:6). Imagine how ridiculous it would be if he said, "I am the career."

Called by God

Once upon a time—in fact, as I sat in that chapel hearing the exact words I had proposed in order to counter the notion—I imagined I would have a ministry career. I thought I would start my ministry with a small church, and hopefully do well enough there to be called by a larger church. I expected to grow my salary over time with good work. Someday I hoped to return to school and then teach in a seminary setting. In short, I thought that my ministry could follow a traditional "career ladder" concept. In 1993, that all looked plausible. It has turned out to be impossible for me.

I made the choice to follow Jesus, which led me out of my first denomination and into the Episcopal Church. I made the choice to enter the sacrament of matrimony with a firefighter from Grand Rapids, which required me to stay geographically restricted to an approximate fifty-mile radius of my adopted hometown. And I made the choice to say "yes" to God's call to me to start a farm ministry, which meant I had to let go of the idea that I would see my salary reflected on the ordinary clergy compensation chart. None of this was part of the career plan path I had in mind as I sat on that hard wooden bench in 1993. But all of it has been part of the way and the life that Christ has called me to, and I would not trade one bit of it for another person's call.

When we give our lives to proclaiming resurrection, we have to be ready for the fact that—like the resurrection itself—our life will take unexpected turns. We make a vow in baptism to allow God to use our life for God's purposes. That vow is fulfilled—or not—day-by-day, moment-by-moment, sometimes hour-by-hour. If we are to fulfill our vows, we must begin with prayer: the kind of prayer that is not simply the repetition of words but the cry of the heart. Beautiful prayers have been written and uttered across the centuries; many are in our prayer book waiting for us. This prayer sums up the point of the religious life in just one sentence:

> Almighty and eternal God, so draw our hearts to you, so guide our minds, so fill our imaginations, so control our wills, that we may be wholly yours, utterly dedicated unto you; and then use us, we pray, as you will, and always to your glory and the welfare of your people; through our Lord and Savior Jesus Christ. *Amen.*[2]

This prayer, sincerely uttered, can change a life. Simply repeating prayers has no impact unless we sincerely *mean* them. We cannot mean them unless we *consider* them. And we cannot consider them unless we take *time* for our relationship with God. God, who gives us every breath that we take and every moment that we enjoy on this planet, surely is more than worthy of any time we can give in return for the time of our lives. We cannot hope to be God's agents of reconciliation, hope, and renewal on this troubled planet unless we root ourselves first in a relationship with God through the practice of discipleship, the reception of the sacraments, the study of scripture, and honest prayer. When we pray honestly to God and offer our lives in dedication to God's purposes, it is amazing what God can do through us.

Plainsong Farm began as a ministry for the renewal of the church and all Creation because God called it into being. As I look back at how the farm began, there is no doubt that the decisive turning point that brought us to life was the answer to one sincere, desperate prayer I offered in May of 2014.

I had been feeling the nudge from God to begin a farm ministry for more than five years. The whole time I had been searching for any-one, anywhere who could tell me what on earth a farm ministry was and show me how to begin. I had consistently come up short. There were no instructions. In 2013 a new book was published: *Soil and Sacrament: A Spiritual Memoir of Food and Faith*. I was so desperate for information about this vocation that I preordered it on Kindle so I could read it the very same day it was published. I remember finishing it in a single sitting, then saying to myself, "Now is the time. I have to begin." And so I did—or actually, I *tried*.

My family and I lived at the property where I felt called to begin a farm ministry. There were ten acres, two barns, and an orchard ready and waiting, none of them in very good repair. "You have to have a farm in order to have a farm ministry," I said to myself. "Start a farm. At least, have a big garden, a flock of chickens, and a plan to expand."

There is not much a person planning to start a farm ministry can do in Michigan when summer is almost over. I pruned some of the apple trees. I ordered twenty-five baby chicks—an heirloom breed—to arrive in the spring. That winter I made a garden plan and recruited friends to help me move sod. In the spring, I cleaned out the old chicken coop. It had more than a foot of debris in the bottom from decades earlier when it had last been used. I pulled out a brooder left behind from the last time the property had been farmed. We rented a sod cutter and moved sod so I could start that big garden. I got the seeds and seedlings planted. I welcomed my twenty-five baby chicks. And it was awful.

I could do the work; I wasn't afraid of work. But I had no joy in the work. My chickens required intensive care a couple times in their first few weeks, and giving that care (for those in the know: pasty bot-tom) did not bring me life. My garden naturally was weedy. Taking out the weeds did not bring me life. I was juggling an active writing life, a ministry position, a family with two children and a husband who worked twenty-four-hour shifts, and this start-up small farm. Every day I had to prioritize my time. Every day I fed and watered the chickens and watched the garden grow weeds. I prioritized writing about the church and talking with people about faith over weeding and tending land. I loved everything else I was doing more than I loved tending those chickens and that garden. I had barely begun, but it didn't take long to feel like a full-scale failure.

It was still incredibly early in the growing season—May 2014— when it became utterly obvious to me that I did not have the gifts to grow a farm. How then could I grow a farm ministry? I had been hearing from God about this farm ministry for almost seven years. How could I stop? Why was God calling me to begin a farm ministry when I couldn't even begin a farm?

Finally in desperation I got on my knees one morning before anyone else was awake. "I can't do this, God," I said. "If you want a farm ministry, you're going to have to do it, because I can't do it. But if you do it, I will try to help."

That was the prayer that started Plainsong Farm.

Not long afterward it dawned on me that the reason we couldn't have a farm ministry was that neither my husband nor I were farmers. And yet we lived on the farm. If it was ever going to be a farm again, it needed farmers: people who *did* find joy in growing gardens and tending chickens, who had the desire and capacity to do that work well. I wasn't that person. For the first time I wondered if *I* was the biggest obstacle to fulfilling the call I felt from God.

Back on my knees I went. "Lord, if it is your will that this place become a farm and a farm ministry, and if our family living here is what is holding that back, then please show us another place to live and we will move there." It was a prayer sincerely offered. And yet not even I expected what happened next. A week or so later, my husband came to me and said, "A new property just listed and I think we should take a look at it."

I had never told him about that prayer.

We went to look. The new house had everything we were looking for in a place to live. We had the capacity to make a bid without selling our old house. Our offer was accepted. As we made our plans to move, I asked my husband if we could keep the old house for a while. He agreed that I could have a year to see if I could begin a farm-based ministry. For a year we would pay the cost of insurance on the house while keeping it vacant, before we would put it on the market. It wasn't even a difficult conversation.

New Life

Only God can give new life. I couldn't give Plainsong Farm life. When I tried, I failed. What made the difference, what turned this farm from death to life, was dedicating myself to God's purposes, seeking God's will, and literally getting out of God's way. To let God bring a farm to life we moved off the farm.

As soon as I knew we were moving, I started looking for farmers. A mutual friend introduced me to Michael and Bethany Edwardson, a young couple who had written out their life dreams earlier in their marriage. (You've read about them in previous chapters.) Top of their list: "Have a farm connected somehow to the church." We took time to discern that our vocations were mutually aligned, identified shared values, and figured out an initial budget and legal structure. Then I handed Mike a key and fifteen thousand dollars and the Edwardsons moved to the farm. Within six weeks they had transformed the property in ways that my husband and I had not been able to accomplish in ten years. They find joy in tending the land and animals and growing food for customers and neighbors; they have the desire and the capacity for this work. I thank God for them daily. They are the farmers without whom there would be no Plainsong Farm.

Plainsong Farm began with a call from God. It continued with my willingness to abandon a traditional career as a clergyperson to embrace a way of life with God. But it only truly began when I said to God, "If you want this to happen, you will have to do it. I can't do it. But if you do it, I will help."

Every Sunday we tell stories about how God calls people, transforms people, and sends people out. Too often we forget that we ourselves are meant to be characters in that ongoing story. We are also people that God calls, transforms, and sends. We reflect on Holy Scripture each Sunday to help us become people who say to God, "What do you want to bring to life? How can I give my life for your glory and for the sake of your people?" All of us are meant to say that. Every single person that God makes, God gifts, and every single person that God gifts, God calls. There is no person on earth that does not have a God-given purpose. Doing small things with great love, as Mother Theresa once said, is probably the most essential God-given work there is. You likely won't know what work God has for you to do until you sincerely pray for it to be revealed to you. Even then, it often takes much longer than you might desire. At least, it did for me.

That is appropriate to my place in Creation. I'm not in charge. All of us are merely helping God with God's great work of the creation and redemption of this world. That's the only real work there is. Our only goal is to align with it. It's so easy to go astray from that work, perhaps especially when we believe we're active in it.

There was no way for the Fords to know on Christmas Eve that the Kitchen Sink Engine would lead to a shifting climate. The Kitchen Sink Engine was just one moment of innovation and creativity. But somewhere along the line, it became evident that the unbridled use of the technologies unleashed in the industrial age was destructive to

God's world. Today the level of investment in the infrastructure of the industrial age is so high, the only way to seek renewal and transformation is through prayer. We need to offer, sincerely and devoutly, the prayer that says to God, "We've failed at caring for your world. We don't know what to do. Will you please show us a way forward?" The only way to begin is by recognizing that we are not wise. We need to relearn what it means to be human on the garden planet we call home.

That's why it's critical for us to pray first and plan second. It's critical for us to recognize that the church doesn't exist to serve our needs for meaning, purpose, and community. The church exists because God calls people to love and serve God. The church exists to proclaim that this is God's world, and we are here to steward it for God's good purposes. If we are the church, we don't just proclaim that on Sunday mornings for an hour a week. If we are disciples of Jesus Christ, we proclaim it with our whole lives. As we say in our baptismal vows, whenever we fall into sin (and I do, every day!) we will "repent and return to the Lord." God knows us better than to think we are perfect. God knows that we are merely mortal, fallible beings—God knows us better than we know ourselves. And God will use our lives if we sincerely offer God our lives to be used.

Planning, Practice, and Stability

Planning is necessary. Without planning, Plainsong Farm would not exist. Seeds have to go into the soil on time; plants have to go into the ground on time too. First and last frost dates must be taken into account for planting out. Irrigation and weeding and harvesting all have to happen regularly. But we also have to respond to the weather of the day, which is beyond anyone's capacity to control. Similarly, our plans for our ministry must be solid and well-considered. But they also need to accommodate the reality that this is God's world, and we are

God's servants. God may have dreams for us that are different from our dreams for ourselves. We may be looking for a career; God is seeking to give us a way of life and salvation. A career can be planned out; a way of life and salvation relies on the Holy Spirit, which "bloweth where it listeth" (John 3:8, KJV). Careers require regular uprooting as the next position and then the next is sought after and attained. But it is hard to proclaim the gospel when you are chasing a job with more pay or prestige. A church organized around careers is a church that has lost the way of Jesus.

Even if you have already started a career, there is always time to have a way of life instead. A way of life—not a career—is what Benedict had in mind when he wrote his Rule of Life, which provided for the practice of discipleship in community by requiring a vow of stability. The Benedictine commitment was to stay at that exact monastery with those exact monks for a lifetime. We may not be called to a lifetime of stability in a single location, but the practice of stability—staying in one place as much as possible—is the beginning of a way of life. It takes decades to learn the story of a place and its people, to be trusted as a member of the community, to build relationships that matter, to care for the ecology of a place with some wisdom. It takes decades—maybe even a lifetime—to learn how to pray for a place and its people well. Holding the intent to proclaim the goodness of the Lord in the land of the living—in one specific place, one local community, working out your own salvation as a visible and incarnate process—shapes a way of life.

I have lived in Michigan for twenty years now and in Kent County for sixteen of those years. This is not at all where I thought I would live when I sat on the hard wooden pew in the chapel at Harvard Divinity School in 1993, being prayed over as I began my first position as a field education student. Back then, I thought Michigan was flyover country and I was hungry for my career to begin. I brought Marvin Bell's words because I needed to hear them. I needed to remember that my life was to be used by God for the glory of God, not for my own glory. In those hallowed halls, the corridors of power and prestige, we bowed our heads in prayer. "Unless the Lord builds the house, those who build it labor in vain" (Ps. 127:1). We prayed that God would build up God's kingdom through us—that we would not get distracted, that we would not fall short. Then we went out to begin our ministry. And though some of us have won awards and gained careers, every single one of us has failed somewhere, somehow. Human nature being what it is, we probably failed in the first five minutes of our work.

In this century, with the church crumbling and the Creation groaning, nobody knows what they are doing. That's the nature of the learning process. What matters is not that we get it right the first time. What matters is that we keep praying, keep learning, keep going. Maybe every generation is the one that leaves Egypt, never enters the Promised Land, but relearns a relationship with God for the sake of their children's future. Certainly we are called to be that generation, to rediscover a way of life in the midst of a world enslaved to greed and death. The good news is that God has already given us that way of life through Christ. Our part in the story is to say "Yes" to God as Mary did. Our part is day-by-day to pray and act for God's life to be made incarnate once more through us. It won't happen according to our plans, though we must plan. It will happen through death and resurrection.

My idea of Plainsong Farm had to die in order for a real Plainsong Farm to be raised from the dead by God. Maybe your church or your project or your ministry will need to die before God can raise it to new life too. That might not be good for your career. But there is no doubt that it is part of God's way of life. We tell that story every Sunday. We are still and always invited to pray our way into our part in that great drama of salvation.

POSTLUDE

FOUNDING PLAINSONG FARM

Plainsong Farm began with a sense of call and a series of prayers: a confession of failure, a pledge to serve God, a request for help. But it also had to take tangible form as a ministry and an entity. It needed a tax ID and a system for financial accountability. It needed legal status. None of these steps were easy. As of this writing, we're working on all of them. Because this is the aspect of ministry innovation that is the most difficult to sort out (at least in my experience), here are some of the details of our story. It is offered in hopes that it may smooth the path of other ministry innovators working on projects that incorporate both Christian discipleship and ecological stewardship. From my faltering missteps, may you find a better way.

In the summer of 2014, not long after I offered the prayer asking God to show us another place to live if it was indeed God's will to bring Plainsong Farm to life, we made an offer on the home where we live now. That offer was accepted, and we set a date to move in the early fall of 2014.

I started looking for farmers that summer. I didn't really know how. Through word of mouth and attending conferences that summer, I found three potential couples who were interested in working with me to begin a farm-based ministry. Only Michael and Bethany already lived in Grand Rapids, and they were by far the most motivated. They were always on time and ready for our meetings. They already had a local network of friends who would be interested in joining the farm as members of our community supported agriculture program. The other two couples were hesitant about the potential risks of moving to the area and failing at a small farm in a location where they had no preexisting social support. They each decided to no longer pursue working with me.

When the other couples dropped out and Michael and Bethany stood out, it was clear that the best way forward was to partner with Michael and Bethany. Then we had to figure out how to create that partnership.

At this time I was the part-time associate priest of St. Andrew's Episcopal Church in Grand Rapids. I was a member of my Diocesan Council and had served on our diocesan bishop search team. From my work in diocesan leadership, I knew that our diocese did not have a mission team for ministry innovation. Our new bishop was completing his first year with us. I had talked with him about the potential for a farm-based ministry when he first arrived in 2013 and received his blessing to try to begin. But I was hesitant to involve the church I served or the diocese in a start-up farm ministry. I thought it too likely that we would fail. (In hindsight, this was a significant failure on my part.) So all I did was ask the Diocesan Council if they would approve opening a line in the diocesan restricted funds for the farm ministry. I didn't ask for any money from the diocesan budget, I just asked the diocese to receive and expend funds, should we receive donations or grants from other bodies. The Diocesan Council agreed to receive and expend funds on our behalf, should we receive them. I wrote a grant request to Province V, my diocese's larger region in the Episcopal Church, but did not receive funding. Still, I had that line in the restricted funds. It would prove critical to our future.

Meanwhile, we had a farm to start. From Farm Commons,[1] a nonprofit legal advisory firm developed to assist practitioners in sustainable agriculture, we received the advice that starting a non-profit farm was unwise. The Farm Commons lead consultant told us that farm products were taxable under IRS guidelines and nonprofit farms were facing pressure from for-profit farms because donations could subsidize low prices, which undercut the market. She told us to create a for-profit entity to hold our farm operation. I knew that creating a new nonprofit was a ton of work, and I was reluctant to ask the church or diocese to cover a completely unproven project, so I took her advice.

Next, I went to a local lawyer, whom I paid to help us figure out how two couples were going to start a farm on one couple's property with another couple's labor. He drew up our articles of incorporation and we started a low-profit limited liability company (L3C). Under Michigan law, this type of entity exists for businesses that have a social benefit purpose. To manage our own family's exposure to risk, my husband and I transferred the farm property to the Plainsong Farm L3C. Our two families shared ownership in the L3C (with my husband and I holding a significant majority ownership), and we wrote a lease agreement between Plainsong Farm L3C and the Edwardsons. By early spring of 2015, we were ready to go. It was just about one year since I had told God I was a failure at starting the ministry that had called me to begin and promised to help God if the farm was brought to life.

The Edwardsons moved to the property and began to turn it into a farm in May 2015. The work they did was extraordinary. Every time I went to the farm something new and amazing had happened: old fence posts were removed, new fences put up, two barns cleaned, old agricultural implements pulled from the fields.

That fall, we were invited to speak at St. Andrew's adult education forum (the church I had served as associate). There we received a question that would significantly influence our early development. "Can I donate food through your farm?" a member asked. We hadn't thought too hard about that question, but when we did, the answer was clearly "yes." By that winter we were ready to begin selling community supported agriculture (CSA) shares. (For more on the CSA model, see appendix E on page 121.) We created a share that was purely for donation and began to develop relationships with emergency food pantries that would distribute our food to their clients. In that first season, donors supported the contribution of 20 percent of our harvest to emergency food pantry partners.

Mike and Bethany more than proved their capacity to farm. That first year they took seedlings into their living room each night because the greenhouse was too small to hold them all. They provided delicious, beautiful food every week in the CSA shares. They communicated with shareholders well and created strong relationships with our pantry partners. By the end of the season, Mike—who had also found time to build and tend raised beds at our closest poverty relief and development agency—had his picture on the wall of a major downtown building as a United Way "People Helping People" honoree. It was clear that God had done God's part in bringing the farm to life: God provided the farmers.

But God hadn't provided the structure. That was all done courtesy of humanity and the law. As winter closed in and we looked at the financial realities of our first year, we agreed that we needed to change our structure. Despite the advice from Farm Commons, it was time to operate simply as a nonprofit. Private donors who contributed shares in the farm to be distributed through food pantries hadn't received a tax deduction because their purchases had flowed through our L3C. That wasn't fair to them and it hindered the growth of that program. In the long run we wanted a farm-based education and discipleship ministry to own the property. That would certainly be a nonprofit entity. We needed to put every resource, every penny, and every effort toward creating and developing that nonprofit entity. By winter 2015, we had received private donations, a contribution from our local hunger walk, and the first installment of a Mission Enterprise Zone grant from the Episcopal Church. Those funds were all sitting in the restricted funds of the diocese. With a successful first year under our belt, I was ready to ask the diocese for more than a line in the restricted funds. I was ready to ask for a partnership.

I asked for time on the Diocesan Council agenda to explain our situation. Council referred me to talk with the bishop and his assistant for finance to figure out a way forward. That conversation led to the recommendation to create and propose a Memorandum of Understanding to Diocesan Council. Fortunately, our CSA included a lawyer who was an Episcopalian. He drafted a Memorandum of Understanding, which was passed by Diocesan Council, and we moved the farm's operational accounts under the diocese. (The Memorandum of Understanding is included in appendix D on page 119.)

By then, I had come to realize that God was calling me to take the last leap of faith and leave my position as a part-time associate priest to focus on developing the farm ministry. We were partnering with Forward Movement to start an online faith formation website, "Grow Christians" (*www.growchristians.org*). We were hosting and developing the Christian food movement website (*www.christianfood movement.org*). My hope had always been to combine on-farm and digital formation that integrated care of Creation with discipleship. It dawned on me that I had my own now-or-never moment. I could likely find another position as a part-time priest serving a congregation, but I might never again have the opportunity to partner with farmers in a farm ministry start-up.

I turned in my resignation from St. Andrew's to be effective in June 2016. It took about five months for me to realize I was at loose ends on Sunday mornings sitting in a pew. Being a supply priest at different congregations around the diocese wasn't right either. Then the small congregation closest to the farm called me to serve God with them—first once a month as supply clergy, then as their part-time priest-in-charge. Holy Spirit Episcopal Church in Belmont now holds the winter office of Plainsong Farm in space that was previously unused during the week, and its members were the core of our first heirloom wheat planting.

Along the way I had begun speaking, writing, and consulting occasionally. I received payment for this work, but couldn't count any portion of that compensation toward my church pension account. As a person in my forties, I was concerned that my leap of faith not impact my retirement any more than it had to. I requested an Extension of Ministry from the Church Pension Group for my independent work and it was granted. This means I am able to contribute, from my earnings, toward my pension. There is nothing about being a start-up farm ministry developer that is good for my financial future. But following the call I hear from God has been good for my soul.

I sometimes think that Plainsong Farm exists because of providence and privilege. My husband and I have the capacity to own a house that brings in no rent while living in another house, mostly just on his income, in this season in our lives while the farm began. That is privilege. But that privilege was not enough to begin the farm. It was God's providence that put together our family, Mike and Bethany, customers, partners and donors, a grant from the Episcopal Church's Mission Enterprise Zone fund, and a restricted line in the funds of the Diocese of Western Michigan. Only God could align this many people and organizations to create a farm that enables access to healthy food for all, environmental education, and faith formation incorporating ecological stewardship.

When this project began, I had never hired a lawyer, talked with an accountant, filed with the state to create a legal entity, created a

Memorandum of Understanding with a diocese, asked for a line in diocesan restricted funds, or sought funding for a totally new project in the community. As this project began, every day I had to do something I had never done before. I usually had no idea if I was doing it right. But I knew I had to go forward if it was going to be done at all. And day by day, God provided me the knowledge I needed for the next task . . . and the next . . . and the next.

So may it be with you.

Study Guide

Can the church move from crisis to renewal? Yes, by reclaiming our core message—that the Earth is the Lord's—and by making God's love evident through prayerful, practical action. The choices we make can build resilience in local communities, share the gospel with future generations, provide healthy food to our neighbors, and mitigate climate change. This is our work, both individually as disciples of Jesus and together in community on our church properties.

Through the saving action of Jesus Christ, we are set free from sin and death to act as stewards of God's good Creation.

Introduction

This study guide is designed to engage a faith community or small group of like-minded individuals to reclaim a role in sustaining God's Creation. It is meant to accompany each chapter for going deeper with the text and concepts within *Resurrection Matters* as well as developing an action plan to move forward, depending on what the participants discern as next steps. The Interlude pieces are not included in this guide, although you may choose to use them to inform your conversations on any of the chapters, but particularly the ones they precede and follow.

As you begin reading this book with others and engage in studying it in greater detail, consider the following:

- What is motivating you to integrate care of Creation more deeply into a life of discipleship?
- Are you troubled by the news about climate change and the decline of the church?
- What are your previous understandings and opinions of climate change, the decline of the church, and/or stewardship of the environment?
- What do you hope to learn and discern for yourself in this study?

Within each chapter section of this study guide, portions of scripture or a quote will be suggested to read and discuss. Having a study Bible such as *The NRSV Access Study Bible* (Oxford), *Harper Collins NRSV Study Bible*, or *Oxford NRSV Study Bible* available to all participants will be helpful, as well as copies of the 1979 Book of Common Prayer. Those who are not Episcopalians may wish to reflect on their own book of worship and denominational documents as additional sources.

This guide can be used in a variety of ways. A group can discuss one chapter at a time with participants reading the chapter in advance. More than one chapter can be discussed per session, choosing one or two questions or activities to focus on. Be flexible to the needs and goals of the group. Practice shared leadership; each person who has this book also has access to this guide. Begin and end with prayer, knowing that God is in the midst of the conversation and silence is part of the process of listening to what the Spirit is calling you and/or your group to do.

Chapter One: Taking Resurrection Seriously

Nurya lays the foundation for her search for answers, reconciling what she believed in, and what she saw occurring in the world around her in the Prelude: Religion Matters and this first chapter. Until adulthood, she had not been part of any organized religion but hungered for something more. She compares her own early experience of searching with that of the church today *and* the climate crisis of our world today.

As you begin this study, share some stories in your group as you build community with one another:

- What do you believe *about* God?
- When did you "find" Jesus?
- What is your history and experience with worship (in a variety of settings) and belonging to a particular church?
- What is the core of your Christian faith?

Read John 20:1–18.

- How does Mary Magdalene *recognize* the risen Christ?
- What does resurrection mean to you? When have you experienced it?
- How do you "practice resurrection"?

Nurya says, "The stewardship of Creation begins with a renewal of religion" (page xiii). She references a number of "documents" to support her statement about the mission and purpose of the Church, including The Five Marks of Mission, noted here:

The Mission of the Church Is the Mission of Christ

- To proclaim the Good News of the Kingdom
- To teach, baptize and nurture new believers
- To respond to human need by loving service
- To seek to transform unjust structures of society, to challenge violence of every kind and to pursue peace and reconciliation
- To strive to safeguard the integrity of Creation and sustain and renew the life of the earth[1]

The Gospel of Matthew is particularly focused on community organization. Read Matthew 16:13–23; the descriptions of "The Church" in An Outline of the Faith (The Catechism) in the Book of Common Prayer, pages 854–55; and Norman Wirzba's quote on page 7.

- What is the mission of the church?
- Is it the same today as it was two thousand years ago? One hundred years ago? One year ago?

This chapter makes clear that Christian faith leads to concern for Creation. Discuss your comfort (or discomfort) in bringing these topics together alongside that of confession, belief, and resurrection.

- What does faith mean to you?
- What's the difference between resurrection and maintenance?

- Do you believe the church is dying? Do you believe the globe is warming? Do you see a connection between the two? Why or why not?
- How do you see your life as a disciple connected to the renewal of the church?
- How are you called to safeguard the integrity of Creation?
- What are you willing to risk or give up for new life?

Chapter Two: The Ecology of Renewal

This chapter begins with the metaphor of a rummage sale applied to the church and its history as used by Phyllis Tickle and Bishop Mark Dyer. They suggest that religion goes through the same cycle of "rise and fall" as other organizations in the history of the world.

- Begin your conversation talking about rummage sales (or garage sales or tag sales—depending on the terminology used in your context of home, neighborhood, or church). What is the purpose of such sales? What is gained? What is lost?
- How has the function of religion as a "meaning-making" apparatus changed over the last two hundred years? The last fifty? The last ten?
- How is your faith/religion "meaning-making" to you today? Is that different than it was in the past? What do you think it will be in the future?

Read Isaiah 42:5–9. God's people have been living in exile, seemingly abandoned by God to their enemies. Isaiah speaks to their "identity crisis," reminding them who God is and how God works. This is the God of Creation, who made everything that is, and who dwells in this wide, open cosmic space, not contained by the cramped space of exile.

Discuss one or more of the following:

- What is the good news that Isaiah brings to the people in exile?
- What were the former things passing away for God's people at that time?
- What are "the former things" for the church (and you) today?

- What is the new thing that you see God doing in the world today? In the church? With you?

As a people of the resurrection, Christians affirm that life comes out of death. Nurya uses David Hurst's theory of organizational life as an ecocycle "loop in which organizational endings are simply precursors to new beginnings—if one is bold enough to take the path that leads from death to life."

- Review the infinity loop diagrams on pages 21–24. Share some examples of where you have seen change take place along the nine points described.
- Draw an infinity loop and determine where your church is and has been on the loop. Where do you find yourself on the loop? Where would you like to be?
- Discuss and define the following terms: exploitation, conservation, creative destruction, mobilization, and renewal. How are they connected to faith and the church?
- How would you describe the difference between the learning loop and the performance loop?
- Compare and contrast: What are the foundational, enduring values of religion? What are the foundational, enduring values of Creation? What are the foundational enduring values of the church?

Chapter Three: Things Fall Apart

This chapter begins with a story about the way Nurya realized how a series of small, precarious experiments carried out across a creative network of people seeking ways to develop a "horseless carriage" could create something new. She cites the kitchen sink experiment by Henry Ford and one early reaction to the new automobile from Laura Ingalls Wilder. Discuss:

- In our own time, what small experiments have ended up vastly changing our culture?
- What type of culture change do you hope to see next in history?
- Are there any small experiments you know about that reflect your hopes?

- What type of kitchen sink experiment would make evident the value of the goodness of Creation as made by God and redeemed in Christ?

In an interview about Henry Ford, a retired curator of the museum he founded described him this way: "He was one of these people who didn't take a job because he knew how to do it. He often took jobs because he didn't know how to do them, and they were opportunities to learn. It's a very gutsy way to learn."[2] Reflect on what you know about the established church:

- Is this an attitude cultivated by the church today?
- Is this an attitude that might enable the church to make the transition from crisis to renewal?
- How might God be seeking to cultivate this attitude within us? Within you?
- What type of small experiment toward the renewal of church and Creation might help you to learn something about your context and possibilities?

Chapter Four: Taking Stewardship Seriously

An American of German descent, Reinhold Neibuhr wrote his famous prayer in the midst of war in 1943 as fascism and conquest barreled through many areas of the world. It was a time of fear and uncertainty, including a strained relationship between church and state as the United States debated whether to enter the fray. It was a time similar to today.

While we are familiar with the short version of the Serenity Prayer, read the full version of Neibuhr's prayer and reflect on it together.

God, give me grace to accept with serenity
the things that cannot be changed,
Courage to change the things
which should be changed,
and the Wisdom to distinguish
the one from the other.

Living one day at a time,
Accepting hardship as a pathway to peace,
Taking, as Jesus did,
This sinful world as it is,
Not as I would have it,
Trusting that You will make all things right,
If I surrender to Your will,
So that I may be reasonably happy in this life,
And supremely happy with You forever in the next.
Amen.[3]

- What is your experience with the Serenity Prayer? Has your past with the prayer focused more on the need for serenity, the need for change, or both?
- What is within your capacity to change? Is it more or less than you wish to change?
- In light of the topic of this book, what can be changed? What should not be changed?
- What property do you steward?
- What resources do you have?
- What do you need to help you move out of your comfort zone?
- When have you turned something over to God? Over to strangers?

Chapter Five: Neighbors Together

Nurya begins this chapter telling the story of when neighborliness went wrong. Then she shares another when it went right.

- Is your church composed of neighbors who live near one another, or does it draw from a large region? How does that affect your life together?
- Who lives in your neighborhood? Your church's neighborhood? Do you know them by name? Do you know what their hopes and dreams are for the future?

- What are some ways your church has created neighborhood relationships in the past? How does that history affect your present life together?
- What are the economics of your neighborhood? What is its recent history?
- What is the "low hanging fruit" in your neighborhood? Is there an existing project, program, or organization in which you already participate to seek the flourishing of God's Creation in your place?
- What happens if you go out into your church's neighborhood and say, "Our church is wondering how we might be better servants of God in our neighborhood, and we thought we'd learn from our neighbors. What ideas do you have?"
- If it scares you to engage neighbors because you're overbooked with keeping the church going, yet your church isn't thriving, what could you stop doing in order to ask that question?

Read Matthew 6:24, Luke 16:13, and Matthew 19:21–26.

- What do these three scriptures have in common?
- What does it mean that you cannot serve God and wealth?
- How is the production of food related to money / the economy?

Wendell Berry states, "Eating is an agricultural act." Nurya adds, "Eating is also a theological act." It's clear that we engage our place in Creation every day by the food we eat. And it's equally clear that we offer God elements from God's Creation on the altar each Sunday when Holy Eucharist is celebrated.

- What is the supply chain for the altar bread and wine your congregation uses for communion?
- Do you know where the grapes and wheat were grown and how they were grown? Do they connect you with your neighbors as well as with God?
- How do our communion practices mirror our awareness and/or neglectfulness of our place in Creation? How might they be shifted to honor God and reflect our role as stewards of God's Creation?

Chapter Six: Pray, Then Plan

While this book is about resurrecting the church in a time of ecological crisis, it is also a book about faith and prayer—putting one's life in the hands of God. Nurya concludes with her personal experience of prayer and the unexpected change that resulted. She shares, "Plainsong Farm began with a call from God. It continued with my willingness to abandon a traditional career as a clergyperson to embrace a way of life with God. But it only truly began when I said to God, 'If you want this to happen, you will have to do it. I can't do it. But if you do it, I will help.'"

- How is serving God in renewing the church part of attending to the earth's ecological crisis?
- How does your prayer life help you find your place as a member of God's good Creation?
- When have you put your full trust in God?
- Do you plan or pray first?
- What will it take for us (humankind) to relearn what it means to be caretakers of the Earth, our garden home?
- How are you called to help God with God's great work of the Creation and redemption of this world?
- How do you reimagine the Episcopal Church (or your own denomination) in ten years? Twenty years? Fifty years?

Next Steps

For your next steps, consider whether you are called to act as an individual or household/family, as a church, or in your wider diocese. Turn to the six-step process outlined in one of the planning processes located in the appendices. Find the appropriate partners and begin.

APPENDIX A

Planning Process for Households

Each household is in different circumstances. That is obvious, and yet it needs to be acknowledged. As you consider how you might be a witness for the resurrection (chapter 1), engage the learning loop (chapter 2), look honestly at the state of the world (chapter 3), take stewardship seriously (chapter 4), be a good neighbor (chapter 5), and put your prayer life first (chapter 6), I suggest you consider taking these steps:

1. **Look inward.** What have your priorities been thus far in life? Are you ready to turn again to God and seek the renewal of your soul, your community, your church, and all Creation? Do you want to make a serious attempt at living the resurrection?

2. **Look around.** Where do you live? Alone or with others? If you live alone, you can make any changes you like. If you live with others, how on-board might they be with any changes you propose? How might you approach that conversation?

3. **Consider your options.** What type of household do you have right now? How far away are you from the church where you worship? What land do you own, if any? How much money and other assets do you steward? How is your health? How radical a change do you feel called to at this point in your life? Based on your options, brainstorm a list of "what I might do next for the renewal of church and Creation." You're looking for options that fit your situation in life, yet also stretch you beyond it.

4. **Pray about what God would have you do next.** It may not be something on your list of options! If you already believe you know what God would have you do, prayer is the right way to begin. The same is true if you don't know what God would have you do. If you don't know how

to pray, find a quiet place where there are no distractions outside you, and try to quiet your mind so there are fewer distractions within you. Offer the Prayer of Self-Dedication found on page 81 and listen. Don't expect an answer right away, but be attentive to your spirit and where you feel led. For more guidance, seek out a faithful layperson, a priest, or a spiritual director.

5. **Settle on one next action to attempt.** If God is already nudging you about a particular project, take a step toward learning how to begin. Don't worry if you don't know how to accomplish it. Learning and growth is part of the process. You may want to reduce household waste, pray the daily office, reduce your carbon footprint, talk to a friend about Jesus, grow your own food, be present in worship every single Sunday, buy a CSA share, or start a garden church.

6. **Find companions.** The best kind are analog, not digital—people who can look you in the eye, bring you soup when you get sick, and with whom you can eat potluck. Second best is social media—which is definitely much better than nothing. With your analog companions, balance task and relationship: care for one another and get something done for God together. Consider the Christian Food Movement site (*www.christian foodmovement.org*) and Plainsong Farm (*www.plainsongfarm.com*) to be among your digital companions.

7. **Keep going.** If you figure out how to do something, share it. If you get a project done, celebrate, rest, and then start another. The whole point of living in a world where the church is in decline and the planet is warming is to find a direction of health and salvation and persevere in that path. You are naturally going against trend lines. If the trend lines were healthy, your work wouldn't be as necessary. Take the Sabbath time God commands and you need to stay in for the long haul. Unless I'm wrong, this isn't about to get easier. But "the one who endures to the end will be saved" (Matt. 24:13).

Appendix B

Planning Process for Congregational Leaders and Church Task Groups

Each church is in different circumstances. That is obvious, and yet it needs to be acknowledged. As you consider how you might be a witness for the resurrection (chapter 1), engage the learning loop (chapter 2), look honestly at the state of the world (chapter 3), take stewardship seriously (chapter 4), be a good neighbor (chapter 5), and put your prayer life first (chapter 6), I suggest you consider taking these steps:

1. **Look inward.** *What assets does your church have?*

   - First, consider the living souls that God has called to make your community. What gifts has God already put among you?
   - Second, make sure your accounting is accurate. Check your balance sheet and income statement to understand how much money your church has. Some projects need money; other projects don't need money. Some projects can even bring in money! But not unless you first understand what money is already among you.
   - Finally, check the boundaries of your land. Try to understand what type of land you have and what might be possible as a witness for the care of Creation. Make sure you know how much land you own and how it is currently being used.

2. **Look around.** *Who are your neighbors?*

   - What do you know of the story of your community?
   - How has your community changed over the past decade? What are the current issues?
   - How do those issues connect with care of Creation and love of neighbor?

- Who is already at work on projects for the care of Creation? Do they have faith partners?
- What is your watershed, and who is tending it? Where is your sustainable agriculture organization? Where is your Interfaith Power and Light? Your Council of Churches?

3. **Consider your options.**

- Is your church ready for a small new project or a big new project? What possible projects did you discover while looking inward and around? What is the energy level for those projects?
- What type of change might your congregation embrace as a natural outgrowth of their previous story of ministry?
- Are you in the midst of a transition or conflict? If so, imagine ways a small project integrating discipleship and Creation care might enhance larger processes of growth and healing.
- Based on your options, brainstorm a list of "what we might do next for the renewal of church and Creation." You're looking for options that fit your situation in life, yet also stretch you beyond it.

4. **Pray about what God would have you do next.**

- Ask for your prayer concern to be placed on the church prayer list. "May X, X, and X, currently meeting together for discernment, discover God's call for them and our church."
- Talk with your worship leaders and ask for their prayer as well. Tell them you are praying about how to renew the church and all Creation. Share some of the insights you have gained from the book. Ask how you can pray for them. Meet together, pray together, and seek God's will together.
- At Holy Spirit, we took time during the worship service to pray about where God was leading us, and invited people to write down their sense of God's answer on index cards. Those index cards helped leaders discern priorities.

5. **Settle on one next action to attempt.** If God is already nudging you about a particular project, take a step toward learning how to begin. Don't worry if you don't know how to accomplish it. Learning and growth is part of the process. You may want to . . .

   - install solar panels
   - pray the daily office
   - take a congregational food audit
   - reduce your carbon footprint
   - begin an evangelism program
   - invite a beginning farmer to use your land
   - be a demonstration site for a watershed agency
   - plant a new congregation
   - close your congregation and provide the space and assets for a new ministry integrating Creation care and discipleship.

6. **Find companions.** If you're reading this in a church group, you have built-in companions. But remember you're tackling problems that are widely shared. Your church is probably not unique in your diocese, and is certainly not unique church-wide. Look for others seeking renewal, whether they are in the next town over or ten states away. Reach out to diocesan staff, read the Episcopal Church's news, find an Interfaith Power and Light or other faith-based group, friend people on Facebook. With your church companions, balance task and relationship; care for one another, and get something done for God together. Invite others in as they show interest. Your group may be exactly the right way for someone to discover the church.

7. **Keep going.**

   - Institutionalize your group as a "group of the church." Give it a name such as "Resurrection Matters," "Christian Food Movement," or "Renewing Church and Creation." Put meetings in the bulletin and invite friends outside of church to any practical earth-care projects you undertake. Rejoice! You started something.

- Then, ask for a line item in the budget. Get on the planning cycle of the church with the rector or senior warden. Integrate your work with other ministries.

- Always be trying to figure out how to do something you don't know how to do yet.

- Know you are never alone. The Holy Spirit has breathed you into existence and whether your work lives or dies, it lives or dies to the Lord (Rom. 14:8).

APPENDIX C

Planning Checklist for Dioceses

Each diocese (or judicatory body) has its own circumstances. That is obvious, and yet it needs to be acknowledged. As you consider how you might be a witness for the resurrection (chapter 1), engage the learning loop (chapter 2), look honestly at the state of the world (chapter 3), take stewardship seriously (chapter 4), be a good neighbor (chapter 5), and put your prayer life first (chapter 6), I suggest you consider taking these steps:

1. **Look inward.** How long has it been since you have engaged in a health and strength analysis of the diocese? If it has been a while, ask:

   - What are your diocese's strengths and weaknesses?
   - Where would you say your diocese is on the cycle of crisis and renewal described in chapter two?
   - Does every church in the diocese mirror the larger trends of decline, or are some churches celebrating adult baptisms and clearly growing disciples?
   - Is any church or ministry in the diocese on the cutting edge of integrating Creation care and discipleship?
   - What processes, if any, do you have at the diocesan level to plant and tend new ministry?
   - Is there any property the diocese owns that is currently going unused, being rented out to an entity that does not proclaim the gospel and make disciples, or being rented to another church that may not value scientific inquiry and the ministry gifts of all the baptized? Please note: if you take a year just answering these six questions, you won't get anywhere. What you want is a quick and dirty analysis, the kind that takes a group of five or six action-oriented

people about a day (with four of the people doing homework in advance to arrive with answers already prepared for questions 3, 4, 5, and 6) so you can move on to . . .

2. **Look around.** Once you get to the diocesan level, your potential partners are state agencies, county health departments, and federal programs. The establishment mentality discussed on pages 66–67 has a definite shadow side, but it also bears gifts. A faith-based organization set up to coordinate multiple projects across a region to benefit communities, especially an organization that is willing to contribute in-kind use of community-facing property, is an interesting partner for multiple entities seeking to advance public health and the health of Creation. Friends, all we have to do is get organized, and that is us. Check the suggested resources in appendix F for potential partners and example projects. This could be one two-hour meeting with the same people having done advance homework. Don't get stuck here.

3. **Consider your options.** This is a tricky thing to do at the diocesan level, because the options may seem practically limitless. What you are looking for is the meeting place of a three-circle Venn diagram: where the strengths and assets of your diocesan community overlap with the needs of the wider region and with the potential to make and grow disciples through honest, neighborly relationship. So, brainstorm your list with those three questions in mind.

   • Given the current strengths, assets, and capacity of your diocesan community, what is possible?

   • What is needed, given the situation of the wider region and the potential for shared work in partnership?

   • What might be effective at making and growing disciples, given what you don't yet understand about that process? (Remember, we're on a learning loop here.)

   • Once you have three lists (and again, don't take a long time with these), see what pops up on all three.

4. **Pray about what God would have you do next.**

- Once you've looked inward, looked around, and considered your options, pray for God's wisdom. The basic mission unit of the Episcopal Church is the diocese, which means that what you choose matters. It also means that every church in the diocese can be praying for wisdom for you. Ask for a special addition to the diocesan prayer cycle. "May X Group, currently meeting together for discernment, discover God's call for one next step for our diocese." Yes, your work does matter this much. And no, asking the diocese for prayer doesn't mean your work has to succeed. Think of the wider diocese as being like Clara Ford hand-feeding fuel to get that Kitchen Sink Engine to life. If you're doing a diocesan-wide learning project, you need diocesan-wide prayer.
- If you have a Daughters of the King chapter or another prayer-focused group, ask them to pray too.
- Most importantly, if the bishop isn't already part of your small group, be sure s/he is on board and praying for you. If you don't know the bishop, but you feel called to seek the health and renewal of the diocese, then the bishop or senior staff want to know you. Make an appointment and ask for prayer and wisdom. You will make your bishop's day.

5. **Settle on one next action to attempt.**

- See if you can identify one small project that will enable you to fail fast and/or learn something.
- Publicize it. The people who prayed for you deserve to know where God has led you. In your announcement about what you are beginning, include a way for others to be involved. Ask them to pray for your next action. Ask them for information and connections. Ask them for what you need (including money, if that's what you need).
- Don't select a next action that is beyond your capacity, though; find one next thing to do that is within your current capacity, but also

grows *you*. Then, see where that small project leads you. If you have chosen well, God will use it to lead you just like Abraham and Sarah were led: beyond and away from what was familiar into new life. You will meet new people, learn new things, engage in new ministry, and feel stretched beyond your capacity. Your project is meant to grow you as a disciple of Jesus Christ. That's how it is supposed to work, and that's why you also need to . . .

6. **Grow in companionship**. New diocesan-level ministries don't go solo for long. The church is hungry for the good news of resurrection to be preached not only in theory, but in practice.

   - As others express curiosity about your work, find a way to inform and engage them.
   - If you are working at the intersection of care of Creation and Christian discipleship, your work is inherently interesting to a wide swath of people. Find a way that these people can come on board as donors, members, volunteers, or more. Let the work of the Holy Spirit touch and engage them as well, and be open to the gifts they bring.

7. **Keep going.** If you started with one, small, doable project that would teach you something and that you could fail at quickly, excellent.

   - Once it is complete, figure out what you learned from it.
   - Figure out what you need to learn next.
   - Figure out what capacity you built through completing that project (even if it didn't work the way you hoped or expected).
   - Go through the first set of questions again, asking: What is possible for you *now*? Ask for more prayers, wisdom, and whatever else you need.
   - At the diocesan level, you may not want to be institutionalized. Diocesan institutions have a ton of stakeholders and they tend to have difficulty letting go or adapting. It's easy to get distracted by

fighting the uphill battle of seeking to become part of the infra-structure of your diocese. That isn't going to get you either health or renewal. Instead, focus on what you can do to make a tangible dif-ference for the health of the people of God and all God's Creation.

- Keep picking one next action, and another, and another, and keep inviting one more person, and another, and another, and God will surprise you with what turns out to be possible. At least, that's how it worked for me.

APPENDIX D

Memorandum of Understanding

This Memorandum of Understanding (MOU) effective March 18, 2017, between the Episcopal Diocese of Western Michigan (EDWM) and the Plainsong Farm L3C (PF-L3C), memorializes the understanding of a collaborative relationship between EDWM and PF-L3C with respect to the creation of a new, emerging ministry in the Diocese of Western Michigan known as Plainsong Farm, located at 6677 12 Mile Road NE, Rockford, Michigan 49341.

EDWM and PF-L3C agree as follows:

Ministry: Plainsong Farm, a new and emerging ministry of the Diocese of Western Michigan, will farm the Property (defined below), as a community-based sustainable agriculture farm, provide charitable food to local food pantries, incorporate worship on location, and provide both online and on-site Christian formation. The priest-in-charge of the ministry is Nurya Love Parish.

Property Ownership and Use: Plainsong Farm is operated on the property located at 6677 12 Mile Road NE, Rockford, Michigan 49341 (Property). The Property is owned by PF-L3C. PF-L3C will provide Plainsong Farm with the use of the property at no cost through December 31, 2020.

Operating Accounts: EDWM will open an operating account in the name of the Diocese of Western Michigan for Plainsong Farm and allow the managers of Plainsong Farm to manage the funds held in the account. The Bishop's Assistant for Finance and Benefits will be a signatory on the account and will consistently have access to accounting for these funds.

Management/Governance: Michael and Bethany Edwardson manage Plainsong Farm, reporting to a board of directors which governs the Plainsong

Farm Ministry. The board shall be initially appointed and subsequently confirmed by Diocesan Council. The names and backgrounds of each board member will be provided to the Diocesan Council each year. The board shall elect a chair, secretary, and treasurer from among its members.

Insurance/Taxes: EDWM and PF-L3C will agree upon the appropriate insurance needs for the property and Plainsong Farm Ministry. All agreed upon insurance and property taxes will be paid out of Plainsong Farm operating accounts.

Development: EDWM and PF-L3C agree that the primary goal is to manage and develop the ministry such that, on or before December 31, 2020, a viable determination can be made as to the renting or purchasing of the property.

Term: The Term of this MOU shall commence as of the date first set forth above and terminate on December 31, 2020. Either party may terminate this agreement by providing the other party ninety (90) days notice of its intent to do so.

Appendix E

Community Supported Agriculture Information

Community supported agriculture (CSA) farms began in New England in the 1980s. They shift the economics of farming by sharing the risks and rewards among a group while also building community in place.

On a CSA farm, members commit to purchasing from the farm at the beginning of a growing season by paying up front for a share of the harvest. Some CSA farms focus on one area (such as vegetables or meat) while others grow a variety of food. There are even some year-round whole-diet CSAs that seek to provide grain, dairy, meat, vegetables, legumes, oils, and sweeteners: a full diet from a single farm. These are very rare; more common is the CSA farm that also aggregates products from other regional farms, enabling members to eat locally and seasonally.

Eating locally and seasonally through a community supported agriculture farm has many benefits, though it is a learning process. CSA farms are usually transparent about their growing practices, enabling members to see exactly where their food comes from. They often offer opportunities to engage directly with the mysteries of Creation by inviting people onto the land to help plant or harvest. And they seek to build community among their members as well as expand their palates through new vegetables, new recipes, and gatherings to share food. CSA farms generally minimize chemical inputs or grow organically, and they often focus on a plant-based diet, making them ideal partners for a congregation seeking their own health as well as the health of Creation.

If you are thinking that a church would be an ideal match for a community supported agriculture farm, you would be right. Many churches serve as drop-off points for a CSA farm, and some even partner with CSA farms to make shares available to members. That's usually as simple as setting up some tables once a week and making a refrigerator available.

The growing edge of church-CSA partnership is integrating the natural cycles of planting, tending, and harvesting into the Christian formation curriculum of the church. Models for this work don't yet exist in the Christian world, although a few experiments are being tried. The Jewish organization Hazon has been working at this longer, and runs a national network of congregationally supported farms by training leaders in congregations to make connections with farmers and then teach Jewish food ethics around the dinner table.

Appendix F

Suggested Resources

PRINT

I. As You Seek a Way of Life

Berry, Wendell. *The Country of Marriage*. Berkeley: Counterpoint, 2013 (reprint edition).

"Manifesto: The Mad Farmer's Liberation Front," included in this book of poems, is a classic. Post it on your wall; read it to your youth group.

Berry, Wendell. *Sex, Economy, Freedom & Community*. New York: Random House, 1993.

I recommend all of Wendell Berry's books; reading him as a new minister was essential to the trajectory my life has since taken. This particular book contains the essay "Christianity and the Survival of Creation," which is important reading.

Chittister, Joan. *The Rule of Benedict: A Spirituality for the 21st Century*. New York: Crossroad Publishing, 2010.

II. As You Seek the Renewal of the Existing Church

Collins, Jim. *Good to Great: Why Some Companies Make the Leap . . . And Others Don't*. New York: HarperCollins, 2001.

Although focused on the for-profit sector, this book provides workable change theory and some key concepts for effective management of organizations in need of renewal.

Dean, Kenda Creasy. *Almost Christian: What the Faith of Our Teenagers Is Telling the American Church*. New York: Oxford University Press, 2010.

This powerful indictment of today's church is a must-read for religious leaders.

Hurst, David K. *Crisis & Renewal: Meeting the Challenge of Organizational Change*. Boston: Harvard Business Review Press, 1995.

The ecocycle model provides a working theory that can help a body move from short-term thinking to a bigger perspective and more possibilities for future ministry. The author reflects on forest ecosystems, the organization of the Quakers, and the shifts in the steel industry. This book is written from a business perspective, but is definitely not just a business book.

Irwin, L. Gail. *Toward the Better Country: Church Closure and Resurrection.* Eugene, OR: Wipf & Stock, 2013.

This brilliant book combines theological reflection, a caring and pastoral tone, and examples of practical action. If you are wondering whether your church can survive, read it together. It will give you both hope and help, connecting the death of your current incarnation to the hope of resurrected ministry.

Kotter, John. *Leading Change.* Boston: Harvard Business Review Press, 2012.

Presents an overview of creating change in established organizations. It needs adaption for the church context, but the insights around motivating and changing behavior are solid.

Tickle, Phyllis. *The Great Emergence: How Christianity Is Changing and Why.* Grand Rapids: Baker Books, 2008.

A concise explanation of the larger forces of history and culture prompting the reevaluation of religious practice today.

III. As You Seek Companions for Practical Action

Bahnson, Fred. *Soil and Sacrament: A Spiritual Memoir of Food and Faith.* New York: Simon & Schuster, 2013.

These stories of four faith-based farms changed my life. Beautifully written, this book offers inspiring examples for practical action.

Heath, Elaine. *Missional. Mainline. Monastic: A Guide to Starting Missional Micro-Communities in Historically Mainline Traditions.* Eugene, OR: Wipf & Stock, 2014.

This slim, practical volume reads like a sequel to *The Great Emergence*. My copy is thoroughly dog-eared.

Lowe, Kevin M. *Baptized with the Soil: Christian Agrarians and the Crusade for Rural America.* New York: Oxford University Press, 2016.

Kevin Lowe does a masterful job of recovering and telling the story of Christians in America who practiced faith through stewarding soil and caring for rural communities.

Sellers-Petersen, Brian. *Harvesting Abundance: Local Initiatives of Food and Faith.* New York: Church Publishing, 2017.

> An amazingly comprehensive overview of food and faith initiatives in the Episcopal Church, with a robust guide for further reading and research included.

Snook, Susan Brown. *God Gave the Growth: Church Planting in the Episcopal Church.* New York: Morehouse, 2015.

> If you are wondering about planting new ministry in an established tradition, this book offers wisdom, guidance, companionship, and help—even if yours is not a traditional church start.

IV. As You Seek Companions in Theological Reflection

Bahnson, Fred, and Norman Wirzba. *Making Peace with the Land: God's Call to Reconcile with Creation.* Downers Grove, IL: Intervarsity Press, 2012.

> Here you will find foundational theology that makes clear the integral relationship between scripture and the care of Creation.

Davis, Ellen. *Scripture, Culture and Agriculture: An Agrarian Reading of the Bible.* New York: Cambridge University Press, 2009.

> A deep reading of Holy Scripture with careful attention to the implications for its meaning today.

Jennings, Willie James. *The Christian Imagination: Theology and the Origins of Race.* New Haven, CT: Yale University Press, 2010.

> This is essential reading for disentangling western Christianity from the mentality of European superiority, a critical and integral part of the church's work now.

Snyder, Howard, with Joel Scandrett. *Salvation Means Creation Healed: The Ecology of Sin and Grace: Overcoming the Divorce between Earth and Heaven.* Eugene, OR: Wipf & Stock, 2011.

> This book takes direct aim at the unscriptural theology that locates salvation in an otherworldly realm.

Sutterfield, Ragan. *Cultivating Reality: How the Soil Might Save Us.* Eugene, OR: Cascade Books, 2013.

> This slim volume written by a young Episcopal priest reflects on the meaning of a life dedicated to caring for a place and its people.

ONLINE

I. Educational Resources

A Catechism of Creation: An Episcopal Understanding (2005): *https://www.episcopal church.org/files/CreationCatechism.pdf.* This resource provides both theological depth and clear analysis of Scripture and science related to the care of creation.

The Episcopal Church House of Bishops' Pastoral Teaching on Care of Creation (2011): *https://www.episcopalchurch.org/posts/publicaffairs/episcopal-church-house -bishops-issues-pastoral-teaching.* To study this pastoral teaching with a group of youth or adults, a leader's guide and curriculum is also available by Jerry Cappel and Stephanie M. Johnson. *A Life of Grace for the Whole World: A Study Course on the House of Bishops' Pastoral Teaching on the Environment.* New York: Church Publishing, 2017.

Eating Together Faithfully: Food that LAUGHS. Life Around the Table, a United Methodist ministry (with help from Plainsong Farm), is developing a curriculum for adult Christian formation incorporating care of Creation through sharing meals, reflecting on scripture, and learning about your local context for ministry. *http://lifearoundthetable.org/curriculum/*

Watershed Discipleship. Biblical scholar Ched Myers and a creative network inspired by his work have created a hub for mutual learning and encouragement, which proposes that this is a watershed moment for humanity and that bioregional discipleship is of the essence. *https://watersheddiscipleship.org*

II. The Christian Food Movement

The website of the Christian food movement contains a directory of books, blogs, curricula, farm/garden churches, and much more at the intersection of care of Creation, food and agriculture, and Christian discipleship. Go to *http:// christianfoodmovement.org/directory/.* This is also a place to share news, events, and short essays.

You can request to add your project to the directory. Doing so makes it possible for us to amplify this work, find one another, and grow this movement. We need a lot more church gardens in there. *http://christianfoodmovement.org /add-a-listing/.*

7. Reprinted with permission from *Crisis & Renewal: Meeting the Challenge of Organizational Change* by David K. Hurst (Brighton, MA: Harvard Business Press Books, 2002). Copyright 2002 by David K. Hurst; all rights reserved.

8. Ibid.

9. *www.cia.gov/library/publications/the-world-factbook/fields/2177.html* (accessed September 5, 2017).

10. C. Kirk Hadaway, *New Facts on Episcopal Church Growth and Decline* (New York: Episcopal Church, 2015), 5, *www.episcopalchurch.org/files/new_facts_on_growth_2014_final.pdf*.

Chapter Three: Things Fall Apart

1. "Origins of The Henry Ford," The Henry Ford, accessed November 13, 2017, *https://www.thehenryford.org/collections-and-research/digital-resources/popular-topics/origins-of-thf/*.

2. John D. Dingell, "Henry Ford Museum and Greenfield Village," The Library of Congress, accessed November 13, 2017, *http://memory.loc.gov/diglib/legacies/loc.afc.afc-legacies.200003161/*.

3. *www.thehenryford.org* (accessed September 5, 2017).

4. Video taken by the author, May 29, 2015.

5. Laura Ingalls Wilder, "What Became of the Time We Saved?" in *Writings to Young Women from Laura Ingalls Wilder: On Life as a Pioneer Woman* (Nashville: Thomas Nelson, 2006), 106.

6. "Sources of Greenhouse Emissions," EPA, accessed September 5, 2017, *www.epa.gov/ghgemissions/sources-greenhouse-gas-emissions*.

7. "3.2 Trillion Miles Driven On U.S. Roads In 2016," U.S. Department of Transportation Federal Highway Administration, February 21, 2017, *www.fhwa.dot.gov/pressroom/fhwa1704.cfm*.

8. Audre Lorde, "The Master's Tools Will Never Dismantle the Master's House," in *Sister Outsider: Essays and Speeches* (Berkeley, CA: Crossing Press, 2007), 110–14.

Interlude: From Denial to Doughnuts

1. Renée Johnson and Jim Monke, "What Is the Farm Bill?" Congressional Research Service, October 5, 2017, *https://fas.org/sgp/crs/misc/RS22131.pdf*.

2. Jon Levenson, *Creation and the Persistence of Evil: The Jewish Drama of Divine Omnipotence* (Princeton, NJ: Princeton University Press, 1994), 12.

3. Kate Raworth, *Doughnut Economics: Seven Ways to Think Like a Twenty-First-Century Economist* (White River Junction, VT: Chelsea Green Publishing, 2017), Kindle edition.

4. Ibid., 25.

5. Ibid., 39.

6. Levenson, *Creation and the Persistence of Evil*, 12.

Chapter Four: Taking Stewardship Seriously

1. For more details about this youth program, please see *https://www.youtube.com/watch?v=vCgme9U92T4* (accessed November 16, 2017).

2. For a completely different, even more unsettling interpretation of this story, see *http://godspacelight.com/2010/05/18/the-parable-of-the-talents-a-view-from-the-other-side/* (accessed November 17, 2017).

3. *http://www.doknational.org.*

Interlude: Meeting Millennials in Gardens and Fields

1. "America's Changing Religious Landscape," Pew Research Center, May 12, 2015, *http://www.pewforum.org/2015/05/12/americas-changing-religious-landscape/*.

2. C. Kirk Hadaway, *New Facts on Episcopal Church Growth and Decline* (New York: Episcopal Church, 2015), 5, *www.episcopalchurch.org/files/new_facts_on_growth_2014_final.pdf*.

3. C. Kirk Hadaway, *Episcopal Congregations Overview: Findings from the 2014 Survey of Episcopal Congregations*, *https://www.episcopalchurch.org/files/episcopal_congregations_overview_2014.pdf*, 2 (accessed March 13, 2018).

4. *Garden to Table: A 5-Year Look at Food Gardening in America* (Willston, VT: National Gardening Association, 2014), 8, *https://garden.org/special/pdf/2014-NGA-Garden-to-Table.pdf*.

Chapter Five: Neighbors Together

1. Willie James Jennings, *The Christian Imagination: Theology and the Origins of Race* (New Haven, CT: Yale University Press, 2010), 2.

2. *http://www.firstcrc.org/#/welcome/heritage* (accessed September 15, 2017).

3. Conversation between the author and Frank Logue, May 4, 2014. Confirmed via e-mail, October 11, 2017.

4. Tikkun, "Nigel Savage of Hazon on a Jewish Food Movement," April 19, 2016, *www.tikkun.org/nextgen/nigel-savage-of-hazon-on-a-jewish-food-movement*.

5. "Jewish Food Movement: Overview," Hazon, accessed October 16, 2017, *https://hazon.org/jewish-food-movement/overview/*.

6. Wendell Berry, "Wendell Berry: The Pleasure of Eating," *Organic Life,* December 10, 2016, *https://www.rodalesorganiclife.com/wellbeing/wendell-berry-pleasure-eating/*.

7. S. J. Vermeulen, B. M. Campbell, and J. S. I. Ingram, "Climate Change and Food Systems," *Annual Revised Environmental Resource* 37 (2012): 195–222. Cited in Rodale Institute, *Regenerative Organic Agriculture and Climate Change,* 21, *http://rodaleinstitute.org/assets/WhitePaper.pdf* (accessed August 15, 2017).

8. Rodale Institute, *Regenerative Organic Agriculture and Climate Change,* 1.

9. Pew Commission on Industrial Farm Animal Production, *Putting Meat on the Table: Industrial Farm Animal Production in America (Executive Summary)* (Pew Commission with Johns Hopkins Bloomberg School of Public Health, 2008), 17, *www.ncifap.org/wp-content/uploads/PCIFAPSmry.pdf*.

10. Tikkun, "Nigel Savage of Hazon on a Jewish Food Movement," April 19, 2016, *www.tikkun.org/nextgen/nigel-savage-of-hazon-on-a-jewish-food-movement*.

Interlude: Finding the Christian Food Movement

1. Lucille Marshall, "Nigel Savage on the Jewish Food Movement," *Movement,* March 5, 2014, *http://www.momentmag.com/food-connection-torah-today/*.

2. Josh Payne, "I Farm 600 Acres with the Help of N.T. Wright and the Rodale Institute. And I Know We Need a Christian Food Movement," Christian Food Movement, March 28, 2017, *http://christianfoodmovement.org/2017/03/28/i-farm-600-acres-with-the-help-of-n-t-wright-and-the-rodale-institute-and-i-know-we-need-a-christian-food-movement/*.

3. Kendall Vanderslice, "Dinner Churches Spring Up Nationwide," Christian Food Movement, January 13, 2017, *http://christianfoodmovement.org/2017/01/13/dinner-churches-spring-up-nationwide/*.

4. Derrick Weston, "It's Time for the Church to See Food as Its Number One Issue," Christian Food Movement, June 17, 2017, *http://christianfoodmovement.org/2017/06/15/its-time-for-the-church-to-see-food-as-its-number-one-issue/*.

5. "Welcome to the Christian Food Movement, "Christian Food Movement, *http://christianfoodmovement.org/*.

Chapter Six: Pray, Then Plan

1. Marvin Bell, "Poetry Is A Way of Life, Not a Career," *The Chronicle of Higher Education*, February 16, 1994, B5. From the author's essay "Bloody Brain Work" in *The Pushcart Prize XVIII: Best of the Small Presses* (Wainscot, NY: Pushcart Press, 1993).

2. "A Prayer of Self-Dedication," Book of Common Prayer, 832.

Postlude: Fouding Plainsong Farm

1. *https://farmcommons.org/*.

Study Guide

1. *https://www.episcopalchurch.org/page/five-marks-mission*.

2. "Henry Ford: Founder, Ford Motor Company," The Henry Ford, accessed November 22, 2017, *https://www.thehenryford.org/explore/stories-of-innovation /visionaries/henry-ford/*.

3. *https://genius.com/Reinhold-niebuhr-serenity-prayer-annotated*.

Acknowledgments

1. "2022 Vision: 7-Year Goals," Hazon, *https://hazon.org/jewish-food-movement /2022-vision-food-goals/* (accessed March 12, 2018).

About the Dedication

1. For more about Anathoth, read Fred Bahnson's article "The Garden Becomes a Protest" *Orion Magazine*, July 1, 2007, *https://orionmagazine.org/article/the -field-of-anathoth/*.

Acknowledgments

I don't know how to acknowledge all the people whose work and prayer has shaped my life and thinking. Despite the fact that the task is impossible, it must be attempted.

Madeleine L'Engle's writing first taught me the potential for Christian faith and scientific inquiry to complement one another. Wendell Berry's work first began to answer my persistent questions about how the world had gone so wrong. Jon Levenson and Sarah Coakley demonstrated that it was not only possible, but also worthwhile to combine sincere intellectual inquiry and devout religious practice. Terry Burke, Betty Ellis-Hagler, Judy Hoehler, and Carl Scovel first showed me Jesus in the flesh. The people of Epiphany Community Church in Fenton, Michigan, honored me by allowing me to serve as their church planter. The people and clergy of Fountain Street Church in Grand Rapids, Michigan, taught me much in my four years as their associate minister.

I give thanks for Jeanine Diller, the first Episcopalian I met who invited me to come to worship with her. I give thanks for the communities of the Episcopal Church in which I began to explore this tradition: Canterbury House in Ann Arbor and St. Mark's Episcopal Church in Grand Rapids. Both accepted me with grace and hospitality when I was still a Christian pastor from the Unitarian Universalist Association. "I was a stranger, and you welcomed me." And I give thanks for the people and communities of the Episcopal Church who invited me to make this tradition my home: St. Paul's Episcopal Church in Greenville—especially John Kirkman, their rector—brought me into the church. John Crean recruited me into the ordination process. St. Andrew's Episcopal Church in Grand Rapids—especially Michael Fedewa, their rector—gave me my first professional ministry role in the church. Holy Spirit Episcopal Church in Belmont is one of the most loving, authentic, and and resilient faith communities I've ever known. I'm honored to serve God as their priest-in-charge. I can tell we're all growing as disciples together.

For many years I felt like I was pressing my nose up against stained glass windows from the outside, trying to figure out how the Episcopal Church actually worked and whether I could belong. In hindsight I am grateful for the time I spent on the outside looking in, because it taught me to appreciate the beauty of this tradition before becoming part of the sausage-making process known as church governance. Now that I have a place in the councils of the church, I give thanks for the Acts 8 Moment of General Convention 2012 that became the Acts 8 Movement of General Convention 2015. Without these church friends, I would no longer have my sanity. Special thanks to Tom Ferguson, Scott Gunn, and Susan Brown Snook who first called for an Acts 8 Moment for the church.

For many years I felt like one of the only people on earth trying to fit together agriculture, food, and faith. I give thanks for Fred Bahnson, Noah Campbell, Ellen Davis, Meribah Mansfield, Ched Myers, Sarah Nolan, John Dempsey Parker, Lisa Ransom, Brian Sellers-Petersen, Nadia Stefko, Norman Wirzba, and other kindred souls who encouraged me before anybody ever put the words "Christian," "food," and "movement" together. By now there are too many such souls to name (although you can look them up at *www. christianfoodmovement.org*).

I give special thanks for Nigel Savage, the founder of Hazon. To quote Hazon: "Wouldn't it be cool if, by 2022, it were clear that a) food was strengthening the relationships between different faith and ethnic communities? b) that faith communities and ethnic communities were strengthening food systems in this country? And c) that the Jewish Food Movement had played a significant and catalytic role in helping all of this to happen."[1] Yes, all that would be very cool. I hope this book is one sign that it's happening.

I am grateful for Tom Brackett, who believed farm ministry was possible before anyone else did. I am grateful for my bishop, Whayne Hougland, whose care and vision mirror the unfailing love of God. I am grateful for Brian Coleman, Emma Garcia, Polly Hewitt, Dana Hougland, Erin Skidmore, Margarita Solis-Deal, and Michael VanderBrug, who make this a west Michigan conversation as well as a national one. I am grateful for Grace Hackney, who invited me into her life and ministry on the strength of one phone conversation and has gone on to bless me with both partnership and friendship.

Curt Bechler of Venture International, who appears in chapter two, hired me for his team while I was in transition between denominations. I will be forever grateful for that, and for everything I learned about crisis, conflict, communication, and organizational renewal from him. It's probably not a coincidence that I was working for Curt when Phyllis Tickle's *The Great Emergence* was published. In many ways this book feels like a sequel to *The Great Emergence*. (Hopefully, one of many.) I only wish Phyllis were here to give her opinion about that. The brief time in which I knew her was a great blessing to me.

I'm grateful for Sharon Ely Pearson, who encouraged me to write about *why* the church would engage in intentional ministries related to climate, food, and agriculture. I'm not sure if I appreciate her more as editor or reassurer -in-chief, but it is certain that without her this book would not exist.

Not one page of this book would be what it is without Michael and Bethany Edwardson. Thanks be to God who brought us together, to Kyle Bos for introducing us in the first place, and especially to Michael and Bethany for being in this work for the long haul. Your presence in my life is an extraordinary blessing.

Finally, because they are the most important, I want to thank my family. My mother supports me even when she doesn't understand me. By doing so, she has taught me more about what family means than I once knew. My husband and children suffered through more time with me typing into a computer and muttering about "the book" than they ever anticipated. Of all the people on earth, I am most grateful for them.

If anything in this book is good, it's because of the work of God. What is lacking in depth, wisdom, or accuracy is my responsibility.

Nurya Love Parish
November 22, 2017
Feast of Clive Staples Lewis

About the Dedication

Cedar Grove, North Carolina, is a small rural community. There, in 2004, Bill King was murdered in the store he owned. At a prayer vigil following the murder, Scnobia Taylor, an African-American descendant of sharecroppers-become-landowners, was moved by God to give land to create a garden for the healing of the community. She chose to give that land to the United Methodist Church where The Rev. Grace Hackney was pastor. Fred Bahnson was hired as the founding garden manager of Anathoth.[1]

Anathoth Community Garden and Farm exists to this day. It is named for the passage in Jeremiah that calls for the people of Israel, in exile, to "build houses and live in them; plant gardens and eat what they produce" (Jer. 29:5).

I was a lonely exile unsure how to begin a farm-based ministry until I read Fred Bahnson's book *Soil and Sacrament*. Fred's book was based in part on his experience at Anathoth. Without Scnobia's gift, that book might not have been written, and Plainsong Farm might still be a dream.

God works in mysterious ways. When I trace my spiritual forebears, they don't just go back through the Episcopal Church in western Michigan. They also go back through a Black Baptist in Cedar Grove, North Carolina, whom I've only met one time, and whose response to a call from God changed my life.